The ~~kickass~~ Guide to Happily Ever After

365 Skills for the Romantic Heart

Kathryn Elliott, PhD

The Kickass Guide to Happily Ever After

Anthetics Institute Press
PO Box 81097, Lafayette, LA 70598
(337) 450-9910

www.anthetictherapy.com
www.facebook.com/Anthetic

All rights reserved © 2017, Anthetics Institute Press

No part of this book may be used or reproduced in any manner whatsoever without payment of licensing fees and receipt of written permission from Anthetics Institute Press except in the case of brief quotations in reviews for inclusion in a print or digital magazine, newspaper, or broadcast.

ISBN: 978-0-9644220-3-2

Printed in the United States of America
To order, please contact:
Anthetics Institute Press
PO Box 81097, Lafayette, LA 70598
Email: anthetics@aol.com

Introduction

We are all at heart lovers. This guide is for you who have found your love and want to keep that love alive. It's also for you who have lost hope. Perhaps when you look at your track record of relationships, it looks like a string of shipwrecks, failures, and just plain bad choices. But in the face of all that, we have one thing to say to you: Your history is NOT your destiny. How can we say that? Because we know that relationships are our grand opportunity for learning. And for growth. I didn't know that before I met Jim. I'd given up on finding a good man. But my destiny was on its way. And it would bring fulfillment beyond my wildest dreams. For 22 years, we shared what we came to call a high-voltage soulmate relationship. It was marked by intense closeness and depth communication; personal growth and heart-stirring romance. Achieving all that took skills.

The Kickass Guide to Happily Ever After was born nineteen years into our journey. Jim suffered a devastating stroke that left him bed bound. Each morning before he awoke, I wrote a blog called Soulmate Skills to share what we had discovered. I would read them to Jim who would agree they were ready for sharing. Jim and I both believed that our fulfillment was more than a personal one. We believe we are to be a sign to you and a guide. On each page of this book, you will find a blog entry I wrote during that time and Jim blessed. We'll be shining the light of everything we learned to illuminate your future path. Whether you're searching for your soulmate or have found your love, may these 365 days of skills guide you into living your own happily ever after.

Love,

Kathryn & Jim

Forever and always, my beloved soulmate, Jim, you are my Prince Charming; my *happily ever after.*

*"When love and skill work together,
expect a masterpiece."*

- John Ruskin

January 1

Your Happily Ever After—An Epic Journey

Have you longed for a great love? Such longing sets us on a path; in fact, an epic journey in our life. Not everyone chooses such a quest. But for those of us who do, it is a journey of self-development and of growth; of fighting your own inner dragons, of individuating from soul-killing relationships. My soulmate, Jim, began searching when he was ten years old. He found me when he was 60. I was 37. We've talked about how we wished we'd found each other earlier so we could have had more time together. But then we automatically realized we wouldn't have been ready for each other before then. Every one of those "questing" years was spent developing into who we needed to be to know what we needed in our mate—and to be able to live out the relationship once we found it. So, take heart. Whether your quest is short or long, each day is an essential growth day for you. We're with you; sharing the powerful skills we learned and you'll need to be ready for your happily ever after.

 # January 2

Where Can I Find My Soulmate?

Where do you look to find your soulmate? The answer is: Wherever your Twin might be. We've found that for optimal closeness, you need to find someone who is so like you, he or she could be your twin. When we say "like you" we mean in values, passions, interests, like-mindedness. So, to find your soulmate, go to places and events you love; that are your passion. Go to them everywhere. That's what Jim did and I did. When he had developed enough to know that his passion was psychotherapy, and that he wanted a colleague, he began looking for his twin at every conference, workshop, and educational program he attended. And that's how he found me at his doctoral program. So, as you get to know yourself and follow your path, there your soulmate will likely be.

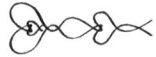 # January 3

Your Own Fairytale Romance

England's princes' engagements are all the news. They conjure in us images of the fairy tale romance we all long for. You can live your own version. I wrote Jim a poem several years ago that captures ours. "It took a stranger to enter the castle, A foreign Knight to break the spell." Here are the elements: a princess under the spell; a foreign knight with a valiant heart; his rescue of her with his chivalrous love. Now, if you think psychologically, you'll realize we're all under a spell. It stems from inner critic messages of devaluation. Many a man is in touch with a courageous, loving heart that longs to set his beloved free. Add the enchantment of falling in love, and there you have it—your own fairy tale romance. Dare to live it.

 # January 4

You're Not Alone

Have you ever felt alone in your quest for a soulmate? Let us assure you that you are not alone. In fact, you are part of a throng! An AARP survey of 2,000 people ages 18-65+, found that the idea of one great love is alive and well: 75% of Americans ages 50 to 64 said they had encountered the love of their life. And 18% said they had encountered a great love several times. What's more, our bodies cooperate in our being perpetual lovers. Rutgers anthropologist Helen Fisher's report of brain scans done on new lovers and long-term loves ages 18 to 80, found that our brains produce the feel-ecstatic neurochemical dopamine whether we're young or old. So, soulmate questers, know that as you seek your soulmate, you are living in the gift of being fully human. You're in good company.

 # January 5

Is There Love at First Sight?

We've had so many long-married people tell us they knew the first time they saw each other that this was the one. And there's no doubt that Jim and I felt that powerful attraction to each other at first sight. But what we say is, even if there is that powerful attraction, you will still have to check two things out: 1) Does he or she meet your criteria? And 2) Your own motivation. Is this attraction *driven* by your replay machinery? Meaning, is this one more pain-filled attempt to get the love you didn't get from your earliest relationships? Once the attraction has passed these two tests, then your love-at-first-sight may well be your soulmate. Now you can welcome the magic.

 # January 6

How to Recognize Your Soulmate

How can I tell if this is my soulmate? You need a list. A criteria list. Your list is something you've been developing for years. It contains all the qualities in a partner that fulfill you in a relationship. Even if you've never experienced a fulfilling relationship, you can know what you want. How? You may have to flip your old partners' qualities. What gave you pain points to the opposite quality that you want in a partner. Write those qualities down. Add to your list. Arrange your list by categories: physical, emotional, affectional, intellectual, spiritual, sexual. Then use your list as a guide to check out a person. Jim had his 56 criteria when he checked me out. He said he would have been happy with 10% of those qualities; ecstatic with 20%. Be he said I had them all. You can have it all too. You need a list.

 # January 7

Is There Only One Soulmate for You?

It's a common question: Is there only one soulmate in all the world for me? Our answer is: We don't know. But what we do know is that you can find and create a high-voltage soulmate relationship. Here are the steps: First, create your criteria list. For someone who is a twin to you—so closely matched in voltage desires, values, and interests that they're like a twin. Second, do what gives you pleasure. There your soulmate will likely be. And if providence or divine intervention happens, accept and be grateful. Third, once you've found that special person, choose emotional closeness and love as primary values. And let those values guide your conversations and behavior. Fourth, use high-voltage communication skills for managing the intensity, honesty, and stuff that will get triggered. Finally, enjoy the bliss. Because, when you follow these steps, you will craft that soulmate bond.

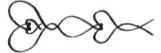 # January 8

Why Seek a Soulmate?

Isn't a good-enough relationship fine? The answer is No, and here's why: Life is going to bring you challenges—challenges that will require every bit of connection between you and your partner. To face the troubles that life brings, the low-voltage strategies of a good-enough relationship, like bypassing hot topics and evading painful issues will result in one thing—distance. And that's painfully lonely. I had to put that to the test. Twenty years into our marriage, Jim became bedbound by a stroke. One day, I was crying alone in the tub. Once out of the tub, I went to Jim and said, "I'm feeling blue. I just want to sob." He reached out his unaffected arm and just held me, while I cried in his lap. I asked him, "Is it alright for me to share this with you? I didn't want to burden you." His wonderful reply: "You always have my shoulder to cry on. Whether the day is bright or grey, you have my heart to rely on" (words from one of our favorite love songs, "Little Things Mean a Lot"). Then he reassured me, "Everything's going to be alright." And with his words, I felt so much better. The high-voltage communication skills of a soulmate relationship will equip you to talk about the feelings and issues that crises bring. And, in the face of the chill of life's storms, to warm each other at the hearth of your closeness.

 # January 9

Your History Is Not Your Destiny

We know; we know. When you look at your track record of relationships, it looks like a string of shipwrecks, failures, and just plain bad choices. But in the face of all that, we have one thing to say to you: *Your history is NOT your destiny.* How can we say that? Because we know that relationships are our grand opportunity for learning. And for growth. I didn't know that before I met Jim. So, I gave up for a while on finding a good man. Little did I know that my destiny was on its way. And it would bring fulfillment beyond my wildest dreams. Jim and I both believe that our fulfillment was more than a personal one. We believe we are to be a sign to you and a guide. We'll be shining the light of everything we've learned in order to illuminate your future path.

 # January 10

Do You Want Closeness?

In order to gain the wisdom your history has to teach you, you're going to need some concepts. The first one we want to give you is *voltage*. It means the level of closeness you want in a relationship. If you long for a lot of emotional connection; talking through your feelings about the relationship, then you want *high-voltage*. If you'd rather a relationship that stays on a surface level—like roommates, then you prefer low-voltage. It's the high-voltage relationship that is a soulmate relationship. It's important that you find someone who wants the same level of voltage that you do. When you think back on your history, you'll find that some, or maybe most, of the failed relationships were because of a voltage mismatch. Here's the secret: Find your voltage match and your fairytale will come true.

 # January 11

The One Essential Ingredient to a Growth-Filled Relationship

"May you have a long life together." That's often the blessing spoken at weddings. But there's so much more than longevity that's possible in intimate relationships. There's growth! And in Anthetic Therapy, we mean a very specific thing by growth: we mean getting free. Free from being driven by your emotional pain and by early rigid decisions. How do you turn a "good enough" relationship into a "growth-filled" relationship? It takes one essential ingredient: psychological-mindedness. What is that? It's valuing using principles from psychology to understand yourself and how you relate. It means being curious about yourself: "I wonder why I did that (for example, got angry, went silent, withdrew, cried)?" So, whether you're seeking a soulmate or are in a current relationship that you want to nurture, make psychological-mindedness your main ingredient.

 # January 12

It's Not All Pretty

I used to think closeness was about the relationship being "all pretty." But I was so wrong. With Jim I learned that closeness is fundamentally about willingness to grow; to confront things in yourself; to change each other as you grow; to heal from old wounds. The gift of a soulmate relationship is that it's transformative. If you try to keep it pretty by not hitting things head on, you end up empty-handed and empty-souled.

 # January 13

Tunnel Vision Limits Our Search

Have you ever been with someone you thought was your soulmate only to find that they were a source of pain, not of ecstasy? Then did you wonder, "How could I have been so wrong? I thought they were the one." Well, here's a concept to help you understand this common mistake: *tunnel vision*. Tunnel vision is happening when we see our partner through the very narrow lens of only one or too few qualities they have. As we develop, we discover and articulate to ourselves, "I want someone who's _____." And based on that narrow criterion, we mistake the person for our soulmate. What's the solution? Widen your lens! And keep widening the lens of your vision. Every day is an opportunity to recognize more and more what you want in a soulmate. It's a developmental process. So, for today, celebrate what you already have learned, and embrace what today will reveal.

January 14

How Will I Know if This Is My Soulmate?

How can you tell if this is your soulmate? One way is by how highly you value the person. If they are on a pedestal in your mind; if you have them high, high in their importance to you, that's a powerful indicator. Why? Because someone who fulfills that soulmate longing you have will be the person who holds transcendent value for you—not just ordinary caring or warmth for them—something beyond that. You look at them and just feel awe that they are in your life.

 # January 15

Mutuality Is the Key

After writing yesterday's thought on valuing your partner highly, I thought, "I need to make sure I've made it clear that the valuing needs to be by both partners." So today I'm writing about mutuality. That means there are two pedestals! Or maybe one pedestal that both partners are nestled together on. So, when you're looking for a soulmate, be sure to check that your partner wants to be with you as much as you want to be with him or her. That you introduce each other with pride to relatives and friends. That you both want a lot of closeness. That's how soulmates are.

 # January 16

Soft-heartedness Is the Heart of the Matter

Soft-heartedness. That's what it takes to live a soulmate relationship. What does it look like: sweet-eyes! Have you ever "made sweet-eyes" with a beloved baby in your family? That's it. You let all the warmth and love you feel bubble up inside and then let it be expressed through your eyes. What does it sound like: doting love words! You let pour forth from your lips all the terms of endearment you feel—like an artesian well of love. What does it feel like: a tender touch. You let all the valuing and awe you feel for your partner be expressed without moderating. Your fingers and hands and lips will touch your partner with the same care you'd give a fine piece of crystal. So, today, let soft-heartedness flow.

 **January 17**

How to Understand Discouragement

Have you felt discouraged about ever finding a soulmate? Ever thought to yourself, "I'll never find that one special person." I know I did. And, at the time, I didn't have the one concept that would have helped me. But I do now and want to give it to you. It's the Inner Critic. We all have one. It's a part of us that not only criticizes us and demands perfection but who also predicts disaster for our plans and hopes and dreams. But you know what—the Inner Critic is not a clairvoyant part of ourselves. It doesn't have the ability to see the future. So, don't believe its negative predictions for an instant. Just label those discouraged feelings: "That's my Inner Critic. I'm not going to believe it." And then, soulmate questers, keep right on pursuing your dream.

January 18

But What If I Get Rejected?

Have you ever thought of taking a risk in looking for your soulmate, and then felt that fear: "What if I Get Rejected?" Well, while that would be painful, the good news is, that's great! Because if you're rejected by someone, THEY WEREN'T THE ONE! How do we know? Because the person who is your soulmate would NOT reject you. Instead, they will value you as highly as you value them. They will want to be with you as much as you want to be with them. And that's how you tell.

January 19

Don't Overvalue Someone Who Undervalues You

Why do people have so much pain in relationships? One primary reason is they stay in a relationship where they're undervalued. That means their partner doesn't treat them as the most important person in the world. Someone else is more important—perhaps an ex or a parent. In fact, there's a long list of people, activities, and institutions that come first. That's fine if you're acquaintances. But it's toxic if you're searching for a soulmate relationship. And notice that we're saying *under*-valued. We're not saying not valued at all. Because, they may value you at some level. And that's what can keep you stuck—settling for crumbs of being valued. So, we recommend this as a mantra for you today: *I refuse to overvalue someone who undervalues me.*

 # January 20

Should You Wait for Your Soulmate or Settle for the First Half-Decent Person You Find?

Have you read, "Stop waiting for your soulmate. Just settle for the first half-decent person you find?" To assess the wisdom of that advice, you have to look at the term *soulmate*. We define soulmate as someone with whom you can connect emotionally at such a depth level that it's at the level of your deepest being—your soul. It's a high-voltage relationship. And that's the heart of the matter. If you long to communicate in a high-voltage way with your partner, "settling" will be a devil's bargain. Yes, you may stave off loneliness, but only to the extent having a roommate would. And, yes, if your primary goal is to birth or parent children, that might work too. But if you want someone with whom you can weather the trials of life, whether small daily rain showers or those tsunamis that life can bring, it's a soulmate who will have the power to see you through those times. And those sunny days—a soulmate will dance with you in the sunshine. That's worth waiting for.

 # January 21

Most Couples Have Only 10% Satisfaction

Are you a 10-percenter? I've been there in previous relationships. I know the loneliness and boredom that come when all you aspire to or can eke out is a ho-hum roommate sort of life with your partner. And I know I'm not the only one. We've found that most couples have only about 10% of the satisfaction that's possible in their relationships. But so much more is possible. In fact, that other 90% is attainable if you have the right values and skills. What values? Beholding for example. And neutral requesting. And we could go on and on. And, of course, we will in this guide. You can start to increase your satisfaction today by choosing to have, not a minimal connection but rather an optimal relationship. We're behind you all the way!

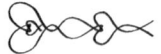 # January 22

Love Is Extravagant

"How many ways are there to express my love for you? I'm trying them all." Jim wrote that to me in 1989. "How do I love thee? Let me count the ways." Elizabeth Barrett Browning wrote those words in 1850. Don't they sound amazingly alike? That's because they were both written by people who were deeply in love. And that's how love is. It's extravagant. It pushes for profuse expression. It has no pride; no stinginess; no holding back. As a matter of fact, it can't find enough ways to speak itself to its beloved. It has no fear of being trite. It just lets loose. So, let us be extravagant with love today.

 # January 23

Love Is a Risky Business

Question: Is love a risky business? Our Answer: Yes! But don't get us wrong. We're not putting it down. Or warning you away from it. Because risk is not the problem with love. It's one of the essential recipe ingredients for love. In order to have a high-voltage soulmate relationship, you have to take risks. Primarily you have to take the risk to initiate; to be forthcoming with your feelings, your thoughts, your stuff for processing. And, of course, if it's a mutual soulmate relationship, your partner will welcome your forthcomingness and will do the same. So, actually, the risk is just an illusion. Because a soulmate relationship is, at its heart, a safe haven.

January 24

It Takes Courage to Be Close

"I need to find a man who can handle me." That was spoken to me recently by a soulmate seeker. And then she clarified, "I want a man who's not scared of what's inside me; who knows it's just stuff." Such important words. They capture a truth about closeness: It takes courage to be close. By this we mean the courage to confront inner material that surfaces with intimacy. Jim taught me this in our first meeting at Asilomar. I told him, "I love that you can bear with pain and other intense feelings." Of course, that takes skill. And that's what Anthetic optimal relationships are all about—the internal skills along with communication skills to bear with stuff as it surfaces and to grow through it. By "growing through it," we mean getting free—having enough psychological distance from any given issue to take executive control of it. It runs both ways—in both partners. That's why my wedding vows included the words, "Jim, I commit to working on stuff—to stand with the pain until we get through to the other side."

 # January 25

Could Mom and Dad Have Been Wrong?

Is it possible that Mom and Dad and all those other authorities from our childhood were wrong about relationships? You bet! I know one of the early things my father said to me was, "Intimacy breeds contempt." In other words, if you get too close to somebody, they'll start devaluing you. Well, only if they're judgmental. And only if they're lacking in empathy. So, I've had to evaluate what my dad said. My conclusion? He was wrong! And if you're going to break free from the dysfunctional beliefs you hold about relationships, you'll have to take those bits of wisdom handed to you by your parents and evaluate them. What might be wrong about what they said? And as you do this, you'll be equipping yourself to recognize your soulmate and to live out your soulmate love.

 # January 26

How to Enjoy Intense Closeness without Losing Yourself

It's a classic problem: Finding that someone wonderful who wants as much closeness as you do; who values you above all others; who wants to talk about your relationship; who wants to work on it. So, where's the problem? You're starting to feel uncomfortable, scared, even smothered. What's that about? It's about the one essential ingredient that will equip you to tolerate closeness—inner freedom. That's our term, and it simply means getting free from your Inner Critic. It's your Inner Critic who's making you feel uneasy; telling you now that you're loved like this, you have to jump through hoops, be perfect, twist yourself in to a pretzel for your partner. So, there's no getting around it. If you want to enjoy that intense closeness, you're going to have to learn the skills for getting free from your Inner Critic. And once you do that you'll be able to revolve around each other like a planet that's just the right distance from the sun—not so far as to be frozen; not so close as to be burned up. You have each other, and you still have yourself.

January 27

"We" Language is Happy Language for Couples

When Jim and I were first married, I found myself saying things like, "*I* need to go grocery shopping." Jim pointed out that there were two of us now—that *We* needed to go grocery shopping. And while this may seem like a little thing, it turns out that *we* language is an essential part of happiness in couples. UC-Berkeley research found that using words like "we," "our," and "us," rather than "I," "me," and "you," was associated with calmer and happier marriages. We've seen this too in our work and in our relationship. "We" language is the language of merging. When we choose deep, connecting closeness, *we*, in some magical way, become one. And that is ecstatic. And transporting.

 # January 28

2 Steps to "We-ness"

So how do you do it? How do you bear being a "we"? It requires two steps: One, an attitude shift. And, two, a values shift. The attitude shift is from seeing yourself as a lone wolf to seeing yourself as part of the pack. The values shift entails moving from rigid self-sufficiency to valuing flexibly merging. So, come in from the cold. Enjoy warming yourself at the hearth of we-ness.

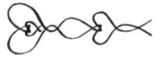 # January 29

When It Comes to Finding a Soulmate, You Be the Judge

This is going to take an attitude shift. If you're soulmate questing, you may have the attitude, "I hope someone picks me." But that's not the way to look at it. Instead, you have to be the one who's picking. You need to be the judge. You, in fact, are The Chooser, not the chosen. What! Isn't that attitude arrogant? Elitist? Absolutely not. Only your Inner Critic tells you it is. Because only you know what qualities in another will fulfill you. Only you know what criteria you're looking for in a soulmate. And only you will recognize your twin. So, soulmate quester, you be the judge!

January 30

It's Your Executive Self Who's the Judge

We're complicated. So, when we said yesterday that you need to be the Chooser, the judge, I need to add something: It's not just *any* part of you that can be the judge. It can't be your little love-starved inner child. It can't be your disillusioned, give-up inner figure. It has to be your Executive Self. That's the part of you who's like the executive of a company—wise, skillful, and who has the company's best interest at heart. A wise executive knows not to hire the angry applicant nor the alcoholic nor the "I couldn't care less; I just need the money" person. The effective executive hires the person who values highly working for this company; who is gung-ho about doing a great job; and who can't wait to get to work. So, it's your inner Executive that you want picking your partner. It's got the wisdom and measured thoughtfulness to recognize your soulmate.

January 31

You Have to Be Your Own Executive Self

If you're going to live from your Executive Self, you'll have to do one essential thing: Get free from hostile takeovers. By that we mean, you may have been living with someone else as the executive authority in your life. It may have been a parent or a spouse, even a brother or sister. As a soulmate quester described it to me, "He'd point, and I'd go." To get free from this pattern, you're going to have to get free from your Inner Critic. It's your Inner Critic that's told you that you didn't have the right to be your own executive. So, here's how to take back your rights: Declare and grow to believe, "I have the right to be the executive in my own life. I have the right to make my own decisions. I have the right to go after what makes me happy."

February 1

Avoid Dead-End Relationships

Navigating your way through the soulmate quest process, you may be spending too much time in dead-end relationships. What can you do? Start asking the all-important qualifying questions right away. Don't wait. Don't hesitate. Some questions you might ask are: "Do you like to talk about feelings?" and "Do you like to talk to your partner about your relationship?" A *Yes* answer indicates a possible soulmate. A *No* answer lets you know this has all the markings of a dead-end relationship in the making. Don't waste your time. Onward with your quest!

 # February 2

Get Free from Your Illusions

Now what if you're in a dead-end relationship? Or have ended one but are tempted to go back? It's your illusions that are the problem. When we have illusions about a relationship that's full of pain and going nowhere, we ignore red flags. We do this thing called "overlooking." We keep hoping for the best. We get stuck doing this, because we hold to a dream—the dream of a profound love; a soulmate love, and that in itself is a worthy goal. But if you're in a dead-end relationship, it means your dream is starring the wrong person as your romantic lead. And that just results in pain. So, hold on to your dream. But let go of illusions. Face the reality that you've miscast the romantic lead. Then you'll be free to find the fulfillment of your dream.

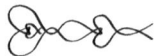 # February 3

How to Make "Never Again" a Reality

After your last relationship ended in heartbreak, you swore, "Never again." Perhaps it was "Never again will I pick someone who doesn't value me." Or "Never again will I stay in a relationship with someone who doesn't want to connect with me." Or even "Never again will I choose someone who won't work on their anger." Yet you may have done little to make that happen. In order to make your declarations of "Never Again" a reality, you'll need to do at least two things: one, get specific with the indicators (the red flags) of the qualities you now are determined to avoid; for example, rage-y eyes indicate a chronically angry person. And two, interview them early on with a specific question that targets the behavior; for example, "Do you value analyzing any feelings of anger?" Do this, and you will be empowered to make "never again" your reality.

 # February 4

Soulmates Pursue Each Other

If you like the sound of *connection*, you're going to have to do one more thing—pursue each other. We mean seek each other out for verbal, emotional, and physical connection. That involves initiating contact; bringing up issues; introducing topics. Pursuing each other is the engine of high-voltage relationships. And it's a mutual process; both partners need to do it. It's fun. So, if you're in a relationship, try it today. If you're soulmate questing, observe potential partners. Are they pursuing you for connection?

 # February 5

Soulmates Feel Awe

How can you tell if you've found your soulmate? One essential clue is that you feel awe at this person. We mean a feeling of wonder at your partner. Amazement at their qualities. You feel fortunate to have found someone you value so highly. In fact, it's a transcendent feeling. Beyond the ordinary. You may have had previous relationships with nice people, but those evoked more a feeling of pleasant friendship. Soulmates are altogether different. They fulfill your criteria for a partner. They have it all. Being with them is an experience in gratitude.

February 6

You Are Each Other's Teachers

Did you know you are a teacher? You are. When it comes to knowing how you want to be related to intimately, you are the expert. So, in a soulmate relationship, each partner is the other's teacher. Jim began teaching me early on how he wanted me to relate to him. He said, "I don't want you to say, 'Don't feel scared;' I want you to say, 'Tell me more about that.'" And I said, "I can learn to do that." My response indicated that I wanted to learn from him. And as we taught each other, we both deepened and grew. So, soulmate quester, be a gentle teacher today. That's the path to your intimate fulfillment.

 # February 7

You Should Try to Change Each Other!

Conventional wisdom is that you shouldn't try to change each other. Forget that! If you live by this maxim, you'll miss out on one of the greatest benefits of a high-voltage soulmate relationship. That is, the gift of growth. Of course, to grow in the way we're suggesting, you're going to need the skill to accept yourself radically. That means you'll need to challenge your Inner Critic at the drop of every bit of feedback you give each other. So, take back your right to be every bit of who you are. As Jim always said, "Come as you are. Be ready to leave different."

February 8

How to Know if He's into You

So, you're into him (or her). How can you tell if they're into you? Easy. They'll ask you interested questions. What are interested questions? They're questions about yourself: what you're feeling, what you think, what you like. In fact, in high-voltage soulmate relationships, you just can't get enough of knowing each other. You'll hear things like, "I want to know everything about you." It's the proverbial "hanging on every word." What if you think they're the one, but they're not asking you interested questions? Find out if they're trainable. Will they do it once you make the request, "I'd like you to ask me questions about myself"? Because if they're really into you, they'll want to know you.

 # February 9

Silence—The Closeness Killer

Silence. Think it's okay? It's not. And here's why. When partners are silent with each other, they're withholding. Because they're, of course, having a million thoughts going through their heads during the silence. But they're not sharing it. And while it may seem normal to keep it to themselves, it's not good for the relationship. That's because the deep-down motives behind silence are often reactive. Fear. Shame. Revenge. Keeping those things inside will produce one thing: distance. So, go ahead and open up. Grope for what you want to say. It doesn't have to be pretty. In fact, the more awkward the better. And once you've opened those hidden places in your heart, closeness will flow. We know. We've put it to the test.

 # February 10

No Topic Is Taboo!

We're serious. No topic is taboo for high-voltage soulmate relationships. You mean, it's okay to talk about my hurt feelings at what my partner said to me? Yes! Well, what about my feelings of attraction to someone else? Yes, that too! Well, what about my fear of their dying? Even that. Isn't that opening a can of worms? Yes. If you want closeness, you have to face the worms. And talk it through. Why does this work? Because your primary value is of each other. And of the relationship. So, any feelings you have are just a blip on the screen of your devotion to each other. Once revealed, those worms just evaporate.

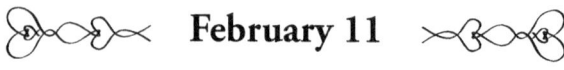

February 11

Do You Really Need Trust?

Trust. It's one of the most frequent issues people come to us with for counseling. Is trust really that important? The answer is Yes, and here's why. If you're aiming for a high-voltage soulmate relationship, you're going to be opening yourself up; laying yourself bare. And you only want to do that with someone who you can trust to be purely loving. Those are jewels you're sharing. You're going to want them to be treated with the tenderness that love brings. So, make sure when you're picking a partner that he or she is a person who values love highly and can easily let love flow. You'll be able to trust that.

February 12

Are Old Assumptions Holding You Back?

Have you heard the one about the tailor and his wife who lived at the back of their shop, worked hard and saved their money and finally had enough to buy a big department store? So, they went to inspect a huge store for sale; looked it over from top to bottom, after which the real estate agent asked, "Well, what's your decision?" The tailor said, "No, we don't want to buy it." On the way home his wife asked, "Why didn't you want to buy it?" The tailor replied, "Because there's no room at the back where you can live." The moral, of course, is that we carry old assumptions into new places and let those assumptions hold us back from moving into those new places. What old assumptions are holding you back?

 # February 13

Here's Your Template for a High-Voltage Valentine (and it's not just for lovers!)

Tomorrow is Valentine's Day, and the commercials for Valentine's gifts are heating up. Dozens of roses! Diamonds! At the heart of what they're advertising is a call to Extravagance. And rightly so. Because love is extravagant. It can't help itself. But even if you're buying roses or diamonds, there's another step to take. And even if you don't have a dime to spend, there's something you can do to express extravagant love. That is: Express your love using extravagant terms. Not good with words, you say? It's okay. We have a map. Jim used it in his first love letter to me, and it melted me. So, here's you template for a high-voltage valentine: 1) When I first met you, I thought _____. 2) After I got to know you, I felt _____. 3) Now, I feel _____. So, go ahead. Fill in the blanks, and let your love flow.

February 14

Yes, We Love Valentine's Day

Well, dear one, it's here! Valentine's Day! We love it! Just think about it. On every other day, the world we live in is focused on the economy, jobs, getting things done. But on this one day, our world pauses and actually focuses on love. And not just a little love—extravagant love. In the grocery store this weekend, I walked through displays of flowers, and what fun, strings and strings attached to balloons! And they all said some version of, "I love you." I want to live in a world where love is everywhere; where no one's afraid to show their love; where it's not the exception; it's what everyone's doing. And on this day, I'm as close to that world as our world gets.

February 15

If You've Thought, "I'm Expecting Too Much"

"I'm probably expecting too much." Sound familiar? You know what that is? It's a thought induced by your Inner Critic. And if you listen to it, you'll believe that you should constrict your life. Pare it down. Don't expect too much. Accept "good enough." Well, don't you believe it. Life has more wonderful gifts to offer than you can imagine. So, dream of your ideal soulmate. Fantasize. Then from your dreams, write down your criteria list for a life partner. You're not expecting too much. Your fulfillment awaits you.

 # February 16

Don't Be Cool!

They'll tell you, "Play it cool! Don't wear your heart on your sleeve. Don't let them see how much you care." That's not what we say. We say, "High-Voltage Soulmate love is honest. Forthcoming. Transparent." It wears its heart on its sleeve. It leaves no doubt as to where it stands. It shows in your eyes. In your words. In your actions. Being cool is for distancing. If you want soulmate connection, don't be cool. Be warm. Even hot! Closeness will be your reward.

February 17

Are There Jupiter People in Your Life?

Are there Jupiter people in your life? Those are people who hold huge power in your mind. They seem to have the same gravitational pull as the planet Jupiter. And the force of that pull leads you to silence your voice; to bend over backwards to not displease them. Maybe it's a parent or a brother or sister or an ex. So, you live in a kind of low-grade fear of their responses to your actions and choices. Can you get free? You bet! And here's how: Realize they only have that power, because you've given it to them. Make a shift by claiming the following releasing statements: "I'm not here to live up to your expectations" and "I have the right to fulfill my deep natural self." Enjoy your inner freedom today.

February 18

How to Handle Others' Feelings

Do you say, "I can't stand it when someone's mad at me," or "I hate it when someone cries"? Well, this may look like you can't handle someone else's feelings, but that's not the problem. The problem is you can't handle *your own feelings* in response to the other person's feelings. If the person's angry, you feel guilty; think you've done something wrong. If they cry, you feel burdened; think you have to do something to make their pain go away. And your feelings are uncomfortable. That's because, what you're feeling is all Inner Critic stuff. Here's what to do: Just listen. Closeness comes when you let other people's feelings be what they are.

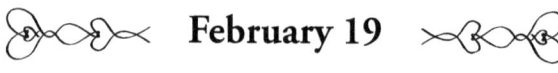

February 19

It's Time to Start Rocking the Boat!

Do you live trying not to make waves in your relationships? Trying not to rock the boat? You know what that is? That's fear. You know where it comes from? From your Inner Critic. Telling you that you're inferior to others. It says what they want is more important than what you want. What they feel is more important than what you feel. You need to fear them. They don't need to fear you. The result? You put others on a pedestal. And you disempower yourself. That's no way to live. We want to experience you in your power. Speaking your voice. Being you! So today, start rocking the boat.

February 20

Beware of This Conversation Stopper

It's called *experience matching*. And it's not only a conversation stopper. It's a closeness blocker. It happens when you say something about yourself, and the other person, instead of responding with a connected response, says something about themselves. For example, you say, "I just met a new guy." The other person says, "Oh, I met three new guys just this week." This is a self-centered response. There's no connecting with the original speaker. And all it gets you is distance. You may do this too. It may seem perfectly normal. A lot of conversation consists of one experience matching after another. And it's why a lot of conversations seem unsatisfying. We want to offer an alternative. It's a communication skill that will produce closeness. It's called *interested questions*. It consists of 7 powerful words: "Can you tell me more about that?" Try it. You'll be on your way to a high-voltage soulmate connection.

February 21

Beware of Humorizing!

You know the couple. They're a laugh a minute. Always chuckling at and ribbing each other. What could be wrong with that? It's the problem of humorizing. That's when partners attenuate the intensity of closeness with a joke. She says, "I heard a song today that made me think of how much I love you. It went, 'Who wouldn't love you? Who wouldn't buy the right side of heaven if you blinked your eye?'" He quips, "You're always wanting to buy something. Heh-heh." Over time, all that ribbing each other starts eroding the closeness they were creating. Don't get us wrong. It's not laughing or joking that's the problem. It's that the joke comes at a crucial moment: the very moment when they could go deeper into emotional closeness with each other. Instead, he deflected it. He didn't meet her. And the closeness got watered down. So, if you want high-voltage soulmate relating, resist the temptation to humorize. That kind of laughter comes at a high price.

 # February 22

Is Love Just a Biological Event?

"What is this thing called love?" We're learning a lot from research about the neurobiology of love—how the brain chemicals dopamine and oxytocin flood our brains during the early stages of love. In fact, when we're in love, our brains respond naturally in ways similar to an amphetamine or cocaine high. It might be tempting to conclude that love is merely a biological event. That conclusion occurs when you limit your world view to a physicalist one; you see all reality as reduced to physical explanations that can be measured and regulated. Not so. Because we are not mere physical beings. If you accept, as we do, that we are also spiritual beings, your world view expands. Finding a soulmate and living out that love is something that transcends the physical events involved in it. We are enfolded and infused with love.

February 23

Is Sex the Bogeyman?

You'd think sex is the bogeyman. At the heart of a lot of messages we got growing up was, "Don't be sexual. It's bad, wrong, dirty, sinful." In fact, my father's maxim, "Intimacy breeds contempt," was code for "If you have sex with him, he'll end up having contempt for you." All this points to how important it is to critique, to evaluate what we learned. And when we do that, we realize sex is not bad. It's our Inner Critic that says it is. And, ask yourself, "Would you have contempt for someone who was sexual with you?" If your answer is no, then our advice to you is: Look for your twin—someone who holds sexual intimacy as a delicious way to express the love and valuing you have for your partner. And then sex becomes what Jim and I have called, "a sexual communion."

February 24

Why Do Women Love to Be Inseminated?

"I want you to inseminate me." Those were the words I spoke to Jim at Asilomar where we met. During the first ten days of our meeting! Have you ever felt about a partner, "I want to have your baby" or "I want you to have my baby?" Well, that's essentially about our longing to merge deeply with someone. But, also important, it's about wanting to introject our partner. That means we admire their qualities so much we want to take those attributes into ourselves and become like them. We do this all the time. It doesn't have to be a partner. It's anyone whom we admire. We don't just copy them; we, at some psychological level, take them inside us. Who have you introjected?

February 25

Don't Miss the Sensuality of Soulmate Connection

Jim had suffered a devastating stroke that left him hemiplegic. I had just come from holding his hand as he fell back asleep. That handholding was a wake-up call for me. My perceptual style is to take in the overall picture of a moment; the tone of it. But that morning, I broke through that pattern into perceiving the details of our handholding. His warm hand embraced mine. Our thumbs were flesh to flesh. Our mounds of Venus were pressed together. My fingers enfolded his thumb. Mmm. What sensuality! I guess his stroke and the limitations it placed on us led me to notice those exquisite details. So, I want to pass on to you what I learned. Don't miss the sensuality in every touch of your soulmate connection. It is a gift.

February 26

Here's the Secret to High-Voltage Sex

It was our first time to make love. And Jim set the tone for it. He surprised me—prefacing our lovemaking by reading a poem to me. It was Phyllis McGinley's "Midcentury Love Letter:" "Stay near me, speak my name. Oh, do not wander by a thought's span, heart's impulse from the light we kindle here. We two have but our burning selves for shelter." It melted me. Those words contain the secret to High-Voltage sex. It's about merging. Your hearts and bodies. And putting it into words. It's letting all the longing that's deeply in us be expressed. Surrendering to each other. Embracing the intensity. There you'll find your intimate soulmate connection.

February 27

Don't Bottle Up Your Feelings

Don't do it! Don't bottle up your feelings. You know why? It's going to hurt you. And it's going to stifle closeness. And one more thing. It will lead to your feelings coming out sideways. In snippy comments. Or outright explosions. Then you'll not only have distance. You'll have wounded distance. See? Nothing good can come of withholding your feelings. But there's a way to do it skillfully. Report it early. And use neutral tone and language: "I'm feeling troubled" or "I'm feeling angry" or "I'm in some pain." That's how you do it. Do this, and you're on your way to a high-voltage soulmate connection.

 # February 28

Soulmates Feel Each Other's Pain

Empathy. You have to have it to have closeness. It means deeply understanding the other's feelings. Feeling the other's pain. One caveat. You have to have the mental flexibility not to get lost in their pain. Because soulmate empathy comes with caring. Jim lived that in our marriage. He said, "Is something troubling you?" I said, "No, I don't think so." But then, he pressed a little further. "You seem troubled. Are you?" And that woke me up to look deeper inside. "Well, maybe it was what happened in a conversation I had today." And darned if that wasn't it! So, your empathy helps your partner confront hidden pain. And then have the love and caring of your soulmate to work it through. So, if you're on your soulmate quest, look for someone who can empathize. If you've found your soulmate, feel the gift of soulmate empathy.

March 1

Is This Relationship All About Me?

Me, Me, Me! It's all about me! These are childlike words that I know well. I had something essential to learn about this in our relationship. While Jim was fabulous at seeing me and meeting my needs, I had to see that there was another person in our relationship. I had a partner who was a real person who wasn't just there to meet my needs. He had needs too. To live a soulmate relationship, you have to grow out of self-centeredness. And you know what? To see your beloved and meet his or her needs feels really good. It's a pleasure all its own.

 # March 2

Want Revenge or Closeness?

Ever turn your back on your partner in bed? Ever refuse to say "thank you" for a make-the-peace gift after an argument? You know what that is? It's a desire for revenge. We want them to hurt like we've hurt. While revenge gives us an initial surge of hard-hearted satisfaction, it ends up being cold comfort. And it robs us of minutes or hours of the pleasure of closeness. So, if our goal is a high-voltage soulmate relationship, we have to make a values choice. Do I want revenge or closeness?

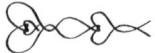 # March 3

Dare to Be Mushy!

Sweetie. Darling. My love. Honey. I could go on and on. They're all love names. And they're what flow when you're in love. You can't help yourself. Because love wants to express itself. To gush. It's an artesian well. Jim and I were early in our relationship when he burst out with our first love word, "Sweetheart." Then he said, "Oh! Maybe I shouldn't have called you that!" but I said, "Oh, no. Call me Sweetheart! Call me Sweetheart!" To an outsider it might sound mushy. But soulmates dare to be mushy.

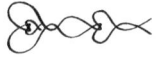 # March 4

Be High-Voltage; Be Happy!

High-Voltage Relating = Happiness. It's an equation Jim and I experienced in our relationship. And we've watched it work for others in our therapy practice. But now research from the University of Arizona supports it. People who spend more time in deep discussions and less time in small talk report feeling happier. We're just built that way. We long for and need connection. We've found the most satisfying way of connecting is to talk to your partner about themselves and about your relationship. Try this today: Ask your partner, "Have you had any thoughts or feelings about our relationship you haven't told me?" Watch closeness grow.

 # March 5

Connect with Each Other's Feelings; Increase Your Voltage

How do you increase the voltage in your conversations? You connect about your feelings about the topic. So, you could actually be talking about the weather. But what will catapult it from low-voltage to high-voltage is to say something like "When it's cloudy like this I feel down." Next, your partner (who's taken to heart our message not to experience match) says, "Can you tell me more about that?" In response, you reveal more about yourself. Then, because high-voltage is about mutual connection, you ask, "What do *you* feel on cloudy days?" Your partner answers. That's how it's done. Connect like this, and your cloudy day will look much brighter.

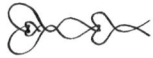 # March 6

Can't Get Motivated? Here's Why

"I don't know what's wrong with me. I just don't have any energy." Ever felt this way? Thought "I just can't get motivated"? Here's the culprit: Your Inner Critic. It condemns the part of you that is full of aliveness and energy for living—your Natural Self. Your Inner Critic calls the plans, ideas, and feelings of your Natural Self "bad, wrong, silly." If you believe that, you squelch your dreams and submerge all that energy for motivating yourself to reach them. So, if you're low-energy today, ask yourself, "Am I doing what my Natural Self wants to be doing or am I doing what my Inner Critic says I should do?" When you start doing what your Natural Self wants, your energy will flow. There will be no stopping you.

 # March 7

Once You Get It, Don't Despise It

At last. Your longing, searching, and waiting are over. You've found your soulmate love. Now, there's one more step. Don't devalue it. Don't treat it as though you despise it. That means, don't focus elsewhere. Don't get complacent. Don't treat your soulmate with contempt. Keep using your communications of beholding and Anthetic listening. In other words, keep fostering connectedness with your beloved. Because soulmate love is a precious thing. Once you get it, reverence it.

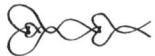 # March 8

Nervousness in Relationships
Can Have Roots in Shame

"Baby! Tsk! Task!" Those were my father's chiding words when he caught a glimpse of the first love letter I wrote in ninth grade. I had written the greeting, "My love…" So, what did I learn from Daddy's response? To feel shame at feeling romantic love for a boy. I had been exposed as loving. For years after that I felt nervous when I was in love; anxious that someone would see me. Perhaps you may have learned something similar too. I know many people who see me in therapy have. Whether it was being shamed by a teacher for passing love notes or taunted by an older relative for holding hands with a new love. Our work in Anthetic Therapy holds that whatever the experience of shaming was, we can get free from that learning. Today, let us liberate ourselves. Let us declare, "I have the right to love; to express my love for anyone freely and boldly!"

 # March 9

Do Soulmates Ever Feel Anger?

What's this? Anger at my soulmate? Can this be? Yes. You are human. And you have stuff. By that we mean emotional baggage from which to get free. And we want to tell you, anger is *always* stuff. It's inner material to work on. Maybe you've been constricting yourself. Maybe you haven't been asking for what you want. Maybe you feel entitled. Whatever is driving it, anger at your partner is not righteous anger. If you see your partner as bad, that's your stuff. In Anthetic couple counseling, we help couples learn to analyze their anger to get free from what's driving it. Because anger doesn't feel good. To you or to your partner. And we don't want you to lose those ecstatic feelings that are part of soulmate love. So, don't trust your anger as the truth. Next time you're angry, say to your partner, "I'm feeling some anger, and that's just my stuff. Bottom line is I love you, and I know you're a good person." Anger needn't sabotage your happily ever after.

 # March 10

What to Do if Your Soulmate Is Angry at You

You're going to need this. Because there will be days when your soulmate is going to be in his or her stuff. Angry at you. Stuck. I speak from experience. And Jim modeled how to handle it. When I've been stuck in anger, fused with a hard-hearted part of myself, Jim did what he called *one-way love*. He just stood in his love for me. And he said, "I'm sorry you're suffering. You don't deserve that. I hope you come back to me soon, because I love you very much." Oh, those words went straight to my heart. And melted it. He saw that underneath my anger was hurt; pain. And he soothed me with his love. That was a profound gift he gave me. So, when your soulmate is angry, do one-way love. It will feel good to you. And may work its magic on your partner's heart.

 # March 11

You're Not Too Needy!

"You're too needy." "You want too much." "No matter what I do, it's never enough." Ever been told this? And did you buy it? Well, we want to set you free today. If you were told this because you love a lot of emotional connection and affection and talking in a relationship, there's nothing wrong with you! You simply like High-Voltage relating. By definition, that means you enjoy a relationship characterized by emotional closeness, deep affection, expressive love, open and honest communication, and more intensity. It actually has a major advantage of producing psychological growth in the partners. So, now you know. You're not too needy! They were a voltage mismatch to you. If you've found your High-Voltage soulmate, enjoy the bliss today. If you're still on your soulmate quest, don't give up. A High-Voltage match is worth waiting for.

 # March 12

The Hyper Nature of Love

Wait till you hear Jim's new idea: He told me that he had been thinking about hyperbolic curves; that is, curves that go on and on. He said, "We've lived that way. Always coming up with new ideas. And we've loved that way. With a love that goes on and on." And when you think about the prefix "hyper," it suggests "greater than normal," an exaggerated amount. And that's how High-Voltage soulmate love is. It's a "mile-high" love; a love that never fails; a love that never dies. No ordinary love. That's what we wanted. That's what we lived. That's what's possible for you too. Go for it!

 # March 13

Love: You Gotta Be Able to Take It or Leave It

Sounds strange, doesn't it? In a book about love! Love: You've gotta be able to take it or leave it! It was one of those startling, turn-you-on-your-head sort of things Jim taught me. So, what does it mean? It means don't value so highly that you'll do anything for it. Like not be honest about who you are and what you want in a relationship. Like hold back from revealing your thoughts and feelings. Bottom line: You have to be free. Free from your Inner Critic should to give away the store just so they'll love you. What we're saying is have your values in the right order. Inner freedom first. Love second. Then you can love freely—and be true to yourself at the same time.

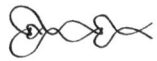 # March 14

When a Solution Is No Solution at All

It started way back when. Since we were little, we've all had to learn to deal with pain. It might have been from neglect or abandonment or abuse. Even good parents fail to meet our emotional needs at times. So early on we had to find relief for our pain. For some of us it was to get tough; for others it was to become extremely tender. On the other hand, we might have become loners or extremely dependent. The problem with these solutions comes when we rely on them rigidly for pain relief. We lose our mental flexibility. And that's when our solution is no solution at all. There is a remedy, however. It's to choose to open ourselves to being fully human. If we're tough, it's to take back our right to be tender. If tender, to take back our right to be tough. So, we wish for you today flexibility. And embracing your full humanity.

 # March 15

How to Correct a Power Differential

"Would you like to eat at that new buffet restaurant?" Answer: "I guess so." Red flag! That answer is a clue that the person is not exercising his or her power. Do you tend to give away your power in relationships? Agree to things just to please your partner? If so, that creates a power differential. That's where one partner has more personal power than the other. It can happen so easily. You love them so much. Don't want to lose them. What to do? The lower-power partner must get free from an inner critic should to defer. The high-power partner must bend over backward to correct the power differential. So, ask yourself, "When I'm in a relationship, am I the high-power person or the low-power person?" If you're the LP start taking back your right to say what you want and need. If you're the HP, ask your partner questions like, "Are you doing what you want to be doing?"

 # March 16

Can You Trust Feelings of Attraction?

It's that rush. You can feel that powerful attraction to this person. But can you trust those feelings? Not by themselves. You've got to put them to the test of rationality. Because feelings of attraction can come from a reactive place. Or from a free place. A reactive attraction is driven. By your past hurt in relationships. It's a place that keeps trying to get it right with the same kind of person who hurt you before. That reactive attraction will only get you one thing—more pain. On the other hand, if you're captivated by someone who meets the soulmate criteria you have consciously set up, that's more trustworthy. As you check the person out further, you'll be rewarded not with pain, but with pleasure.

 # March 17

Is Finding Your Soulmate a Matter of Luck?

A lucky charm. Is that what it takes to find your soulmate? Don't bet on it. When Jim and I met at Asilomar Retreat by the Sea, it was for us a culmination of a focused soulmate quest. Plus living true to our deep self by pursuing our doctorate. And a good sprinkling of determination to seize the moment of our meeting. But we must admit, it felt like something bigger than we were had a hand in bringing us together. So, whether you're searching for your soulmate or have found your love, here's our wish for you: *May your mind be clear, your heart be true, and may all the Good there is bless you with your heart's desire.* Happy St. Patrick's Day!

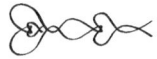 # March 18

How to Know if Your Behavior Is Driven

How do you know if your behavior is driven? If your attraction is one more heartbreak waiting to happen? If your responses to your partner are relationship-wreckers? Here's one essential clue: Is your behavior easily interruptible? Driven behavior is not. It's like you're in a trance. What you have to do is come to a screeching halt. Take back your right to take your time. Then introspect. What am I doing? Is what I'm doing likely to lead to pain or fulfillment? You can do this. We want you to be free.

 # March 19

You're Going to Need Affect Tolerance

Being in a high-voltage soulmate relationship sometimes feels like you're standing in a strong gale of emotions. That level of intimacy means you're having and talking about powerful feelings. Another term for feeling or emotion is *affect*. To live out such a relationship, you're going to need *affect tolerance*. That's the ability to bear disappointment, emotional pain, anxiety, and loneliness without being overwhelmed. It also means the ability to confront and accept feelings of sexuality, hostility, passivity, and aggression in yourself and in your partner. You're going to need skills for this. One skill we want to offer you is an Inner Critic challenge: "Just because I experience strong feelings doesn't mean I have to do a damn thing." Try it! You'll feel your inner strength and freedom grow.

 # March 20

In Order to Grow, Ask Yourself Why-Questions

Some people say, "Feelings just come and go. Nothing you can do but wait till they pass." That's not what we say. In Anthetic Therapy, we recommend you see the opportunity for growth in the feelings you have. Growth will come as you do *introspecting* about those feelings. Introspecting means looking within. Asking yourself why-questions—and answering them. For example, "Why am I being defensive?" and "Why am I being judgmental?" As you answer these questions, you'll discover the subconscious machinery that's clanking away, driving your behavior, and blocking you from creating your High-Voltage soulmate relationship. So, today, turn inward and ask away.

 # March 21

Don't Say, "I'm Not Your Mother"

"I'm not your mother!" That's what some people say to their partner who's asking for nurturing or soothing. But that's not what High-Voltage soulmates say. Why not? Because we revel in being multiple roles for each other. Mother. Father. Daughter. Son. Friend. Priest. Here's why it works: When you love and care about your partner, you enjoy the complexity of meeting each other's needs. But you keep one important concept in mind—*mental flexibility*. You don't get crystallized in any one role. You fluidly move among roles: One moment the mother providing comfort and soothing; the next moment the daughter needing admiration and love from daddy. One moment the friend providing a listening ear; the next moment the priest being the source of assurance from a loving god. It's an expansive—and fulfilling way to live your relationship. Here's to flexibility—and a deeper intimacy.

 # March 22

Present Your Soul to One Another

It's a beautiful Native American love charm, "Your soul has come into the very center of my soul, never to turn away." Jim and I were doing that soul-bonding early in our relationship. And that means revealing ourselves without disguise or mask and providing an enfolding place for that revelation. It's a profound experience. If you're with your soulmate, you can create that sort of merging. If you're soulmate questing, look for someone who is open to a soul-bond.

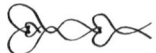 # March 23

Soulmates Don't Blame Each Other

She said, "People said we couldn't sustain happiness, but we are." I asked, "How do you account for that?" Her answer: "We talk a lot. About everything that's going on between us. And if something one of us is doing isn't going right, we know it's never ill-intended. I don't see him as having malice." Wow! That's the right attitude. Because seeing each other as the enemy will erode a relationship. And blaming each other will kill it. So, keep monitoring your attitude. Because soulmates don't blame each other. They see each other as a good person.

 # March 24

What to Do Instead of Blaming

Did you take to heart yesterday's guidance to stop blaming? And are you wondering, "So now how do I stay connected when I'm upset?" Here's what to do: *Vulnerability Talk*. It's talking from the layer of feelings that are underneath your negativity toward your partner. Vulnerability talk includes talk about your fear, hurt feelings, feeling gypped, guilt feelings, and neediness. They're the kinds of feelings our Inner Critic typically condemns as weak. Vulnerability Talk is not for sissies. It's often scary and requires heroic bravery. But it forms the solid and courageous foundation for a High-Voltage soulmate relationship. You can use it as a test too. If someone zings you for vulnerability talk, they've just flunked your test. So, soulmate quester, be courageous! Do vulnerability talk. It's essential for your happily ever after.

 # March 25

Wake Up to Every Little Thing

"Every little thing you do I notice. Notice and take delight in. Even your unlatching my seat belt in the car." Those were words Jim wrote me in an early letter. They remind me that there is exquisite pleasure in being sensitive to little moments of connection; of niceness; of love; of beauty. We sometimes let our senses get dulled. So, soulmate lovers, take in every little thing today about each other. Then speak it. And soulmate quester, add sensitivity to your criteria list. Live today awake to love and connection.

 # March 26

Soulmates Don't Trash Their Partners

It's morning coffee time! And it's got me thinking about the kaffeeklatsch. Sitting and sharing a cup of good coffee and connected conversation with our friends is such a warm, wonderful time. It's one of our favorite things. If you like this too, just beware of one danger—the temptation to get into grousing about your partner. Complaining about him or her. Pretty soon you've worked yourself up into a snit. Whoa! This is the person you love that you're talking about. You want to treat them as the highly valued person they are to you. With respect. If you're upset with your partner about something, talk directly to your partner about it. Process your stuff. Make requests. In other words, turn *to* your partner, not away to others. Because soulmates don't trash their partners.

 # March 27

Celebrate Your Partner's Triumphs

"I did it!" When your partner says that, it's time to celebrate. Whether it's a major triumph or a minor one, you can connect with your partner by celebrating. It means empathizing with your partner's feelings. And then joining them. You'll say things like, "Wow!"; "That's wonderful!"; and "Tell me the details." And don't hold back. In fact, gush! Yes, gush! Let your joy in your partner's victory well over. Don't miss this pleasure. It feels great for both of you.

 # March 28

Don't Be Guided by Fairness

"Would it be fair to ask for this?" That's a common question we're asked. We say, "Don't be guided by fairness." That will lead you into a swamp of bookkeeping in your relationship. You'll end up thinking things like, "They're asking for too much!" or "I shouldn't ask for this." Instead, ask for *everything*. But tell your partner, "Please do it only if you freely choose." Now, you're being guided by inner freedom. And that's an essential ingredient for high-voltage closeness.

 # March 29

How to Produce Closeness

Plop! That's the sound a rock makes when you throw it into the water. Then all returns to silence. And it's also the term we use for a particular communication gap. You know when you've said something and the other person is silent? Plop. In order to produce closeness, you'll need to avoid plops. Instead, come to grips with what your partner says. Not use clichés. Not respond to only part of what your partner says. When you respond in a thoughtful way, you'll produce involvement. And closeness. That's the essence of high-voltage soulmate relating. And it's one more test for you to use in your soulmate quest. When I speak to this person, does it produce plops? Or do I receive an involved response?

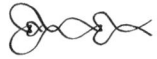 # March 30

How to Handle Relationship Bloopers

You know you've done it. If not, you will. It's those relationship bloopers. You say something negative on impulse to your partner or friend. Maybe you said it out of anger. Or frustration. Or disempowerment. And once you've said it, you see the hurt it triggered in your partner. And you feel the distance between you that your comment caused. You wish you could take it back. But of course, you can't. So, here's what you can do. And it's so simple. You say to your partner, "That was just my stuff." And that's the truth. Because negative comments really aren't about your partner. They're about you and something that's going on inside you. Once you look at it, that blooper can blossom into freedom. And growth.

 # March 31

High-Voltage: The Path to Transformative Growth

Lagniappe. It's a Cajun word for "something extra." And, boy, do you get lagniappe from a high-voltage relationship! Because when you use the high-voltage skills we teach—like feedback, honest communication, and beholding—you're going to wind up with not just a close relationship. You'll have transformative growth. When your partner expresses not only what they love about you, but also what they don't like about you, you'll see things in yourself that you'd never see alone. And they'll be things you can benefit by changing. So, enjoy your lagniappe today.

April 1

Does Romance Have to Decline?

Does romance have to decline in relationships? Absolutely not! In fact, romance can *increase*. You'll have to work this from two angles. One, clear away any barnacles of negativity that arise. By barnacles, we mean those feelings and attitudes of anger, resentment, revenge, and withdrawal that partners can get into. Talk about them. Analyze them. And two, create romance. Through touch, words, events. Then savor them. Jim and I have a binder with lists: "Our Top 5 Enchanted Meals"; "Our Top 5 Vacations"; and "Our Top 5 Sexual Experiences." We've often read them over, talked about them, and savored them. And you know what! It was romantic all over again. The romance kept flowing, even to Jim's passing. Follow our lead. Romance can increase for you, too.

 # April 2

Flirtation Does Not a Relationship Make

You gotta love 'em. Those flirtations. A look exchanged. A touch of the hand. A quickening of your heartbeat. They can be the first step in a soulmate relationship. But sometimes that's all there is. How can you tell if it's *only* a flirtation? One thing will be missing—involvement. Deep emotional connection. So, don't equate flirtation with involvement. Flirting is fun. Like cotton candy. Sweet. A treat. But you can't live off it.

 # April 3

Flirting Is Just Step One in Soulmate Connecting

"I hope I'm not invading your space." Those were the first words I ever spoke to Jim. I had walked into the meeting room; he alone was sitting there. Fourteen other empty chairs. I sat in the one right next to him. As I placed my briefcase on the floor, it fell over onto his leg. That's when I said those words. But, of course, I *was* invading his space. And his response? "Not at all!" (He told me later he was thinking, "Invade my space! Invade my space!") That was the right response. Welcoming. Here are the elements in our flirtation we want to teach you: 1) If you see someone you like, initiate. Be the first to speak. 2) Make your words high-voltage—something personal and direct. (I didn't say, "Nice weather.") Include your feelings. 3) Evaluate their response. A high-voltage soulmate response is direct, enthusiastic, welcoming; not lukewarm, and never dismissive or judgmental. Follow our lead. Your flirting will be step one in your soulmate connection.

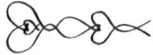 # April 4

Should You Play Hard-to-Get?

Remember those teen slumber parties where advice was doled out with great import? Or maybe you had a man-to-man talk with an older brother. And the advice was, "Play hard-to-get. They'll want you more." Well, some interesting research out of Stanford University found that the old advice was only partially right. If something is hard to get, you may want it more. But once you get it, disliking it will set in. We have an idea why: Playing hard-to-get is not genuine connection. It's the opposite. The message of the distancer is, "I'm of great value. You're not worth connecting with." And once you get such a distancer, you realize you've gotten someone who undervalued you. So, if you're wanting a high-voltage soulmate relationship, indicate your welcoming and valuing of each other from the start. Don't play games.

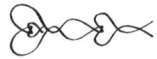 # April 5

How to Handle the Problem of "Looking Easy"

So, if you follow our advice to not play hard-to-get; instead to be welcoming and connecting right from the start, won't you run the risk of looking easy? The short answer is Yes. But here's how: You *are* easy. Easy to connect with. Easy to have a high-voltage involvement with. Remember, you are the judge. It's your Executive Self that is checking out whether this person wants high-voltage connection just like you. If they are judgmental or contemptuous of your offer to connect, they're not the one for you. It's a mismatch. You are powerful. You decide whether to pursue a relationship with this person. Do they pass your test of welcoming you tenderly and lovingly?

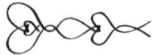 # April 6

Initiate, Soulmate Quester!

"A friend will *initiate* a hug. You don't have to do anything; will say, 'I'd like a hug.' And will seek you out. And will be concerned if a meeting is not forthcoming." Those were notes Jim wrote to himself during our initial meeting. He was reminding himself of criteria for a high-voltage soulmate relationship. And he was observing my behavior. I was passing his tests, and I didn't even know what they were! That's how it goes when you've found a twin. You *want* to initiate just as much as the other person wants you to. And, of course, the initiating is mutual. You're like puppies, falling all over each other to play!

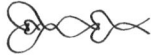 # April 7

You Have Thrusting Power

You have thrusting power. Man or woman, you have it. It's the power to go forth into your life and to fulfill your dreams. We believe it comes from a spiritual place within us. A place in the structure of who we are that is a nexus between God and our humanity. And it is where the divine energies of love and power issue forth. It's an artesian well, always flowing. So, today, dream your dreams, open yourself to those energies, and from your freedom thrust forth!

 # April 8

Separate Yourself from the Herd

Being part of the herd. The family herd. The schoolyard herd. The workplace herd. That way of life feels comfortable. But it comes at a price. The price is your own unique individuality. There's another option. It's to *individuate*; that is, to become free. Free to think your thoughts; to feel your feelings; to dream your dreams. Progressively free to access the potentials inside yourself; then to deploy those potentials whenever you choose. So today try giving up your herd mentality. Who you are is a gift to the world. And we want to know you. What's more, your soulmate will want to know you too.

 # April 9

Go for Your Ideal

"You love me as the ideal of how I want to be loved by a man." I wrote that to Jim in the first six months of our relationship. I had never expected I could find anything close to the ideal man. In fact, I had given up. But you know what! It didn't matter. He came anyway. As I lived my life, risking to go where my Natural Self, my deep self wanted to go, he was there. So, I say to you, follow your heart. Do what lights sparks for you. And be open to the one who fulfills your ideal of how you want to be loved.

 # April 10

Is Your Armor Clanking?

Most of us do it. As children we put on a suit of armor. It was to defend ourselves from pain. The pain of our Inner Critic. And the pain of others' rejection of us. So, we armored ourselves with looking cool, not giving a damn, distancing. Or with being so helpful and loving that they wouldn't see we were in pain. Now, as adults, that armor is clanking away in our relationships. And causing all sorts of problems. But you can dismantle the armor. Piece by piece. By challenging your Inner Critic messages. As you become free, it may feel awkward at first. You might even experience some anxiety. That's normal. You've been cramped in that protective suit for years. We want to assure you such feelings will pass. And you'll run free.

 # April 11

Why Won't He Commit?

Ever found yourself loving someone who just won't commit? And you spend hours trying to understand. On the surface, it looks like he (or she) is just stuck in a marriage they really don't want to be in. Or involved with someone else. Or wanting to play the field. Or unable to leave their parents. But beneath the surface is where you have to look. Inability or unwillingness to commit to you is usually driven by two things: 1) They are fused with the other person. Emotionally attached. Would feel too much pain if they stopped. 2) They undervalue you. They don't see your worth and value it highly enough to want to commit to you. So, given all this, why do you stay? That's driven too. By your Inner Critic and your blackhole. Your black hole longs for love (as do we all). Then your Inner Critic says you're not worthy of someone who values you enough to commit. And it adds, if you give up pursuing this person, you'll never find anyone "as good." Today, you can step back from all this. See the underpinnings of your pain. And good news: Get free! We recommend you use this challenge: *I have the right to a relationship with someone who values me so highly they want to commit. And Inner Critic, you can't predict the future. I refuse to trust your predictions that I won't find anyone as good.* We're supporting you all the way.

 # April 12

How to Stay Calm in a Flood of Feelings

It's gonna happen. That flood of feelings. Whether from the excitement of packing for vacation or preparing for a wedding. Or those challenging moments of dealing with a health crisis or a negative encounter with someone. I watched Jim deal with his stroke for three years—numerous hospitalizations, encounters with strangers, even life-threatening moments. And through it all he maintained amazing equanimity. Here's how he did it. He lived a psychologically principled life. That means he chose to not automatically give in to whatever pressures he was feeling. Instead, he told himself, "This feeling is just a feeling; not a fact." He told his Inner Critic, "I have the right to be right where I am. I'm still a good person. Just because I experience strong feelings doesn't mean I have to do a damn thing." And he chose to use rational thinking instead of emotion-driven impulsiveness. Those principles are the foundation for a high-voltage soulmate relationship.

 # April 13

"I Don't Want Any Negative Feedback"

"I don't want my partner to tell me what he doesn't like about me or my behavior. I just want to be loved." What's the matter with that? Well, it will lead to a chain of events: "I can't tell her what I'm not liking that she does." That leads to not talking. Which leads to distance. Net result: The closeness you so long for is lost. And it was a matter of attrition. Add to that net loss one more thing: The unique opportunity for your own psychological growth is lost too. One warning: Don't think we're recommending that you accept negativity such as anger, judgmentalism or sarcasm. We're not. When your partner tells you what he doesn't like, he must say it lovingly. Here's how Jim did it in his 1989 letter to me (I had sent him a Valentine cassette with my favorite music): "While I was listening to the first two numbers, I was transported by ecstasy; Kathy's music! Her gift to me of herself! But then the vocal stuff I found a bit of jangly, and I thought, oh my god, I can never tell her that! I just won't say anything. No, I can't do that; I've got to tell her." And he did. And so, I learned what he liked and didn't like. I knew him better. We were closer in a new way: Not by virtue of liking exactly the same things, but because we were more transparent with each other. I knew him. He knew me.

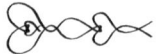 # April 14

The Problem of Dandruff in Relationship

Dandruff: A spot of spilled food on your clothes. Walking around with your zipper unzipped. Each is an occasion for embarrassment. Even shame. We want to help you get free from the psychological mechanism that drives such feelings. First, know that embarrassment occurs when some secret "defectiveness" inside you is exposed. Your Inner Critic pounces with a jolt of shame. Now that you know that, you can challenge your Inner Critic. "Just because I have dandruff doesn't make me less of a person." "I have the right to spill food on my clothes. In fact, I have the right to splatter food all over myself." "I have the right to walk around with my zipper unzipped. I'm still a good person." The point behind these statements is to stop believing your Inner Critic messages. To no longer base your self-worth on Inner Critic values. Now, here's the relationship piece. If someone is judgmental toward you; if they zing you with a put-down look or statement because of your imperfections, that's their stuff. We recommend you say to yourself, "I'm not here to live up to your expectations of perfection!" If you choose, ask the person to work on reducing their judgmentalism. If they're not willing, place them on your list of people not to have a close relationship with.

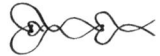 # April 15

What Takes a Fifth of a Second?

What takes a fifth of a second, gives you a rush like a cocaine high, and touches your heart? Falling in love! It happened to us too. I walked into that meeting room the first day of my doctoral studies. Saw one man in profile. In a split second, took in his intelligence, his beauty, his wisdom. Thought, "He looks like a psychologist; probably wouldn't be interested in me." Responded to the first part of my thought; ignored the second part. Walked straight to the chair next to him and sat down at his left hand. I never left his side. That fifth of a second changed my life. So, if you think the time is passing slowly until your beloved comes, in a fifth of a second, your soulmate will appear.

 # April 16

Baker's Dozen: May Be Love Addiction

The Baker's Dozen: when you give something extra. In relationships, always giving something extra may be a clue to love addiction. Here's how it sounds: "I have to offer something extra to get people to like me. I can't just be myself." Here's how it looks: You offer something to keep people attracted to you. Could be money, gifts, sex, listening to their complaints, letting them live with you. Or perhaps walking on eggshells, not making requests, not challenging what people say. Here's how it feels: Angry. Resentful. Used. Taken Advantage of. Now we want to tell you what drives such love addiction: Your Inner Critic. It tells you you are so defective, no one would want you just for you. It adds that if you were to assert yourself, they will surely go away. You'd be all alone. So, you pretend not to be angry. The solution? Get free from your Inner Critic. Here's a good place to start: "Inner Critic, I have the right to be what you call defective. I have the right to assert myself in relationships. People who value me will not go away. Those who don't value me don't belong in my life anyway."

 # April 17

Help for Your Personal Growth

"The turmoil you feel is a good sign. It means that some old patterns are dying and are fighting to stay alive. And that new ones are being born. Whatever happened to open you up, to deepen you, to expand you will call you to a new destiny." Jim wrote this to me in 1989 as I went through cataclysmic changes. At that time, I was getting free from old patterns of disempowering myself in order to please others. Perhaps you are going through a similar process. We know it can feel scary, even lonely. If so, be encouraged. You are our fellow strugglers. As Jim said to me, "Yours is the natural struggle of a person in an exciting and painful growth process." We cheer you on.

 # April 18

Are You Contentious?

Quibbling over little details: "No, it was 6:30, not 6:00." Arguing scrupulously over minute points: "You wore your blue shirt, not your grey one." That's how you can tell if you're being contentious. If you're witnessing it, it's tedious. If you're the target of it, you'll feel weary. If you step back and take a look at what it's doing to your relationship, you'll see that it's killing closeness. Somewhere along the years of our relationship, I found that I was being contentious. I was driven by my Inner Critic to set the record straight; to care more about getting it right than about communicating with Jim. If you want to stop this pattern, monitor your pull to be argumentative. Then tell yourself, "I'm not gonna go there." For even more freedom, you can add, "I have the right not to set the record straight." You'll choose closeness. Like me, you'll find that it's infinitely more satisfying.

 # April 19

Cheating: How to Protect Your Relationship Against It

Cheating wreaks havoc on hearts. So, why do over half of men and women do it? According to a Reuters report, the ability to communicate, empathize, and bond have a lot to do with it. While genes may create vulnerability in these areas, the good news is those qualities can be learned. We know. It's our specialty. In our therapy practice, we teach couples how to create such a deep emotional bond that they're protected from infidelity. We call it High-Voltage relating. Its hallmarks: everyday thrilling emotional intensity, feeling talk about each other and the relationship; passionate, creative sexuality; lots of affectionate touching; valuing each other above all others. When couples are absorbed in each other in such a connected, empathic way it fulfills them so deeply that no one else could hold a candle to what they have. The best news is that High-Voltage relating can be learned. We teach the skills you'll need. We're committed to helping you create soul-fulfilling fidelity.

 # April 20

Shy? Don't Let It Silence You

Kathryn: "Sometimes I think you are shy about saying things directly to me" Jim: "Oh, yes, I am! And then you miss out on the good things I have for you, and it's not fair." We wrote these things to each other one month into our relationship. Jim understood the impact his being shy could have on our connectedness. He added: "Please complain whenever I do not give you the fullest contact, with no punches pulled, from my heart." With this invitation, I asked from time to time, "Are you feeling shy right now?" True to his promise, he took that as a wake-up call to put into words what he was feeling. It kept us close. We recommend this to you. When you're feeling shy, don't let it silence your voice.

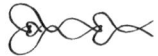 # April 21

Is "Sweetness & Light" Sabotaging Your Closeness?

Are you into S&L? That's short for "Sweetness & Light." You've chosen to value "niceness" and "politeness" over closeness. You don't dare say the truth to your partner. Now I love tenderness, which is good. But that led me to slip into a pattern of not being honest. Not telling Jim what I really felt. Why does this happen? Because if I were to have been honest, my Inner Critic would plead me guilty to the crime of rudeness. Honesty sounds rude to your Inner Critic. But it's absolutely essential for a High-Voltage Relationship. Don't get us wrong. We're not saying you should be uncaring. You can be honest in a caring way. S&L will get you distance. Honesty is a first step to closeness.

 # April 22

The Trouble with a Standard Relationship

He: "What's the matter?" She: "Nothing's the matter!" He: "Something's wrong; I can tell." She: "For God's sake, stop bugging me." Slam! Exit! This dialogue is the stuff of the Standard Relationship Model. It consists of not being honest. Not revealing what you're feeling. Definitely not being forthcoming. Its intention is to prevent arguments and fights. The trouble with a standard relationship is that it reaps a harvest of distance. Multiply that one distancing conversation times five or ten years, and you've got a divorce. Or, if still together, a life of quiet desperation. We want to offer an alternative: The High-Voltage Relationship Model. It's our original concept. It consists of a skill-based way of relating guided by honesty, forthcomingness, and processing judgmentalism. It reaps a harvest of closeness.

 # April 23

Here Are Your Love Verbs for The Day

Jim and I love words. We each tested 99th percentile on the language portion of IQ tests, so words are meat and drink to us. As I read through our love letters today, I realize there were categories of words we used that expressed our love in warm and wonderful ways. The category we want to share with you today is Verbs. I'll quote how we used them as we wrote each other: "You *core-touch* me by what you wrote." "You *warmed* me with what you said." "I *treasure* your words." "Shall I *tell* you what you mean to me?" "Here are things I *value* you for." As you can see, you don't have to test at 99 to use these words. They're simple, yet powerful. They're your love verbs for the day.

 # April 24

Are You Connecting?

A key ingredient to happily ever after is found in the communication style of the partners. It's called *connected responding*. A connected response occurs when the responder's responses are directly connected to what the speaker has said. An example: Speaker: "When would you like to leave?" Responder: "7 pm." In contrast, disconnected responses are tangential, defensive, evasive, and irrelevant. Disconnected responses create distance. Connected responses keep you close—for a lifetime.

 # April 25

What If My Soulmate Is an Alcoholic?

You say: "I believe I've found my soulmate. He connects with me, beholds me, supports me. He's everything I have longed for. However, he is an alcoholic. When he drinks, he no longer connects with me. What do I do?" We say: How wonderful that you have found someone who connects with you deeply. This is a case of a block to living out your soulmate love. We call such an impediment "reactivity." Addiction is one form of reactivity. As you're experiencing, when the addicted person is under the influence, they are no longer relating to you from their Natural Self. Instead, they're relating from a reactive inner figure. The solution: getting free from the reactive inner figure, "The Addicted One." You can call your partner to this freedom. They will most likely need help—through some form of recovery program. Once free, they and you can fully enjoy your soulmate love. Our best wishes to you and your partner for that fulfillment.

 # April 26

Let's Go to the Heart of the Matter

What is the essence of soulmate love? It's 'communion.' That's what we've experienced. It's sharing yourselves at the deepest level. A union of souls. Jim and I noticed that as we revealed our feelings, longings, thoughts, and beholdings of each other, there was an undeniable sense that God was in it with us. Watch for this as you either search for your soulmate or live out your soulmate love. You will have that experience that you're connecting soul to soul. And God will be there too.

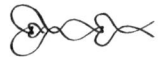 # April 27

How to Never Get Bored in Your Relationship

"This is one of the things I love about you—that nothing you do is ordinary, it is charged with meaning, and I merge with them, from the jasmine soap to the unbuckling of seat belts! Oh, what a rich life we have here, with so many things full of significance; it's like a rich and exotic feast." I'm quoting from Jim's letter to me in February 1989. His words contain the recipe for how to never get bored in your relationship. Here are the 3 ingredients: 1) Imbue everyday items and activities with significance and meaning. For example, Jim sent me a bar of jasmine soap as a gift, because he knew I liked sweet smells. It arrived on a day when I had received news of a friend's death. Seeing jasmine as a healer of the heart, I took the soap and created a shower ritual. I wrote Jim, "I used your soap and received the healing, love and blessing I knew you intended toward me." 2) When you see your partner making meaning of ordinary things, do what Jim did—behold it with sensitivity. Tell your partner that you see what they are doing. 3) Merge with your partner about this. Empathize. Join them in the wonder of the moment. This recipe will not only prevent boredom, it will create as Jim said, "a rich and exotic feast."

 # April 28

Can You Put Limits on Love?

"Every day I think of you and sense my love for you, and it feels stronger and deeper than I have ever loved before, and I think: This is as deep as I can ever love; there is no room for any more of it; I've reached the absolute limit. And then you say or do something, and I get a rush of even more love for you, and I think What could I have been thinking? So, I realize that I can't put any limits on how much I love you; there will always be room for more, impossible as that may seem at any one time." This quote is from Jim's letter to me in 1989. What he was realizing we found to be true about love. You can't put limits on it. It just keeps coming, more and more. Why is this? We experienced that it's because the source of love is God. And God's love is limitless. So, our encouragement to you is, if you think you've reached the end of your love, go to the source. There's always more where that came from.

 # April 29

Do You Splatter in Conversation?

Do you have difficulty addressing the topic of the conversation? Do you struggle with speaking impulsively, without thinking first? We call this "splattering." It involves talking in a disconnected way—by giving your own associations to the topic. Why do you do this? It's because an inner figure, the Regressed Little Kid comes on stage and takes over. When we're in that old childlike state, we can't engage in focused thinking, and so we can't speak in a focused way. Want to know what's deep down driving this? It's our attempt to avoid the humiliation of an Inner Critic attack if we were to be honest and direct. Knowing this, you can work free of it. How? By challenging your Inner Critic. Here's an example: "I have the right to answer directly and honestly, even if you say it's the wrong response, Inner Critic!" There, of course, is more, but this will get you started. You'll be free to relate on a Grownup level. And that feel so much better.

 # April 30

How to Recover from a Broken Heart

This is for you who have had a broken heart. I've thought, "If Jim dies before me will I have a broken heart?" Then I thought, "No, that doesn't fit. Because I have been loved fully and totally by Jim. Nothing held back. I've been seen by him to the core. And his love for me and his impact on me will never die." Instead, I think I will have a grieving heart. To me the term "broken heart" implies that you've loved and been rejected or abandoned. So, given that definition, how do you recover from a broken heart? First, you feel the pain and cry. Then, you take stock. You step back and say, "Wait a minute. I'm not going to put my self-esteem or my happiness in the hands of someone who doesn't value me. I'm going to give my energy to having pleasure and to making connection with those who do love and value me. I'm going to take the vacuum that's been created and fill it with new love." There's nothing like love to heal a broken heart.

May 1

The Voyage of Soulmate Love

"I have gotten on a raft of some sort that was floating down a small gentle stream, and it was very pleasant, and I could get off wherever I wanted. But then the stream widened, and the water got faster-moving, and now I must steer carefully to avoid the whirlpools and rocks, and it takes all the skill I have, and I love it. Now the stream is so wide that I couldn't disembark if I wanted to, and for an instant I feel trapped. If I am trapped, it's a sweet precious trap that brings forth much goodness in me like no other trap!" Here Jim was musing on our relationship, the journey on which it was taking us. It was one we had both longed for and awaited for many, many years. Once embarked upon, it had us in its grip. It held us there for 22 years and still holds. Whether you're waiting on the bank for your soulmate or whether you've stepped onto the raft, or even if you're traveling the rapids together, we can promise you: Soulmate Love is a voyage worth waiting for.

 # May 2

Sleepless Night? Could Be Backlash

We hope you slept well last night. But in case you didn't, here's something that might help: Your sleepless night might have come from "backlash." That's a term we use in Anthetic Therapy to mean the pouncing of your Inner Critic after you've gotten free enough to perform some action that defies it. You might feel guilty, ashamed, anxious. It's all Inner Critic emotional punishment of you for stepping out of the box it put you in. Here's what to do. Say one more releasing statement that goes like this: "Just because I felt bad doesn't mean I've done something wrong." You should sleep better tonight.

 # May 3

Your Actions Form Soulmate Bonds

Bond: The attractive force that holds together the atoms of a crystal (Webster's Dictionary). Jim wrote in 1989 to me, "I want to tell you about the bonds I feel we are forming. Strongest of all was your pledge of loyalty to me. Almost as strong was when you came to my room, sensing that I was feeling bad. Oh, how important that was! And there are many little ones, each important. When you brushed against my arm. When we hugged at the airport, and you pressed your full body against me. And, of course when you said you wanted to spend the night with me. And when we actually did." As soulmate questers, you form bonds too. In both large and small actions, that attractive force will hold together the two of you. It will be as beautiful as a crystal.

May 4

Soulmates Are Risk Takers

Kathy: "Can I really be close to him? Can I trust him? Dare I ask him for things?" Jim: "I want us to take even more risks--say things about which we might think, 'Oh, I couldn't say that!' Risk making mistakes. Risk triggering stuff in the other person (because we're willing to work on it if it comes up)." How do soulmates do this? By a commitment to talk about their feelings. Jim continued: "Now, if you ever feel uncomfortable with anything I say or write, I want you to tell me. I'd like an agreement from you that you will tell me of any negative reactions you have. Okay?" So, I did. And, because I risked, and he risked, and we talked about our feelings, we got more and more closeness. And you will too.

 # May 5

When You're Doubting the Goodness of Your Life

I discovered this thought tucked away in a binder. It's something Jim said to me on a day when I was discouraged. I want to share it with you: "When you're doubting the goodness and purpose of your life, because of sickness or other challenges, remember: Your life has been a flow of your own efforts at fulfilling your Natural Self + miraculous interventions by the Universe (in my case meeting Jim at Asilomar). My life is being watched over and guided by a powerful benevolent force who opens windows of opportunity at amazing times. There is a Divine Order, and I am in it." We hope this encourages and comforts you, as it does me.

 **May 6**

You Call Each Other to This Love

On the surface of your relationship, it looks like sweet love. Beneath the surface, there is more going on. Much more. In fact, you are calling each other. By this we mean evoking feelings, attitudinal shifts, and behaviors you'd never touch if it weren't for your partner's influence. Jim explored this concept in his June 1989 letter: "We are calling each other to great things--greater depth, greater merging, greater union. We each call the other to surrender to the love that wants to flow through us and give it its strongest voice possible. We call each other to inclusive growth--I to include my shamed child, you to include your pain-filled little girl. And we are each growing into what we are called to be and do. It will be difficult for a while, but soon we will have the results of these callings as a foundation upon which to deploy and exercise our personal power in the world." We wish for you the sweetness of the surface of your love and the growth invoked when you follow your lover's callings.

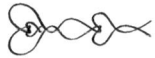 # May 7

Glitchwork Gives Us Power

Glitches can have a curious benefit to soulmate partners. A glitch is a strained communication, even an argument, over stuff either partner is having. You'd think it would harm the relationship. And, of course, if left unprocessed, it certainly can. But, Jim and I discovered the gift that a glitch can contain--power. Jim wrote it this way: "Our glitchwork gives us, ultimately, more power. Power to confront a negative feeling in the other. Power to trust. Power to soothe our little child parts, as they feel scared by the high voltages of our relationships." We were using the skills Jim had developed with his groups. And they were serving us well. Skills like asking each other, "What are you feeling?" and "Can you tell me more about that?" Try them. And watch your love and power grow.

 # May 8

Protect Your Relationship

Have you noticed that not everyone supports your relationship? Some want to chew it up. That was Jim's and my experience before we got married. We had to stand strong and defend our relationship against those who were critical of either of us or of marriage in general. We had to realize that some people have hardened their hearts against love. In the face of their attitude and comments, you have to tap your inner strength. Stand for your beloved and your relationship. Protect each other.

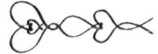 # May 9

Come Out of Your Cave

"I have to go into my cave. I need to unwind; to decompress." Some people live this way. It's destructive. Here's why. It prevents closeness. And we've discovered, in nine out of ten cases, it's to avoid feeling humiliated if you were to expose what you did, felt, or thought. What to do? Choose openness. That means readily and voluntarily self-disclosing your thoughts and feelings to your partner. Instead of silently withdrawing into yourself, you say something like, "Someone at work said something insulting to me today, and I couldn't come up with a retort." With that in the open, you can now get free from your Inner Critic: "I have the right to freeze and not know what to say. I'm still a good person." And as you talk with your partner about it, you'll be close. That's the warmth of high-voltage relating. So, come out of your cave. It's lonely in there

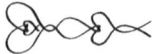 # May 10

Are You Expecting Too Much?

You've probably heard people talk about marriage with low expectations. Don't buy that. Know instead that you can dream big dreams for your relationship. And you can make them come true. I watched our wedding video recently to celebrate our anniversary. The words my mother said to us I want to pass on to you. "I bless you with love and gentleness. And wonder. And remember: When love and skill work together, it creates a masterpiece." Take your love and passion, add skills for producing closeness. There's your recipe for fulfillment. Serves two. Can be shared with the world.

 # May 11

Sexy Secret for Upping the Voltage

Want to up the voltage in your intimate relationship? Here's a sexy thing Jim and I always did that we want to pass on to you: Sweet Nuthins! Those are soul-touching intimate phrases or sentences or questions that you reveal to each other. Then you huskily whisper them to each other. It's dynamite. So, think about what you want to hear at your deepest level and tell each other, like Jim did in his April 1989 letter to me, "Here are things I would like you to say to me…"

 # May 12

What is a Soulmate?

Soulmate. It's a word many of us use. It's a primal longing. We want to offer a definition. It's the one we guide ourselves and our work by. In our work in Anthetic Therapy, a high-voltage soulmate relationship is one where you connect at the core depth level—the level of soul. It means going as deep as you dare with each other in surrendering to openness, to verbal connectedness, to honesty, to cherishing. If you want a lot of emotional closeness and talking through your feelings, you want a soulmate relationship. It takes skills, like beholding, requesting, extravagance. That's what creates the magic. We've forged the way. You can have this too. Our love is with you.

 **May 13**

When You Find Your Soulmate, You Find Home

"Remember waking up in the night, hugging each other, your soft flesh curving into mine, fitting together as though God had made them for that purpose?" Jim wrote that after our first sexual communion. I've often thought about how perfectly we physically fit together. The image I have is of a pinball falling right into its hole. I'd never felt that "rightness" before. It was like coming home. And we're not the only ones who say that. We've heard other people say, "Anywhere you are is home to me." That seems to be another thing to look for in a soulmate: Do I feel so comfortable, so safe with this person that it feels like I have, after a long journey to distant places, found home? If you have been blessed to have found that, savor it today. It is a gift.

 # May 14

A New Way to Overcome Defensiveness

Do you find feedback from your partner hard to handle? I did. Jim had to teach me a skill for responding to feedback. I'm passing it on to you. Instead of getting angry or defensive when someone tells you something they observe about you, for example, "Are you feeling angry?", you can say, "Not that I'm aware of. Let me think about that." Equipped with this skill, you can stop automatically rejecting feedback. Once you look at yourself with this attitude of curiosity, you can expand your self-knowledge-and your self-acceptance.

 # May 15

How to De-Trance & Live the Life You Want

Are you going to hypnotize me? That's a question people have often asked me when they come to me for counseling. My response always is: "No. I'm going to de-hypnotize you!" Because we all tend to walk around in a trance. It's a spell cast by your Inner Critic, who tells you you're defective, worthless, shameful and inferior. What is needed then is a dehypnotizing process. You can throw off the trance under which you have been living. As you challenge your Inner Critic, your Natural Self will take heart. Who you are deep down will begin to emerge. So, begin to take back your rights from your Inner Critic. Today, awaken to your preciousness and power.

 # May 16

Caring is at The Heart of Soulmate Love

Good Morning greetings. Holding doors open so your partner can pass through. Saying "Excuse me." These are the little civilities and courtesies that caring is made of. And it's motivated by empathy and sensitivity for your partner. We propose Anthetic caring. That's caring that expects no return. It's done for its own sake. Because it gives you pleasure to be sensitive. It is the essence of genuine considerateness, politeness, respect, and courtesy. And it makes everyday life together a warm hearth. If you're soulmate questing, look for someone who treats you with caring. If you're in a relationship, treat each other with caring. It will make your house a soulmate haven.

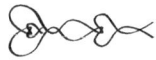 # May 17

Sweeping Issues Under the Rug Doesn't Work

We know it's tempting to sweep relationship issues under the rug. We call it "Bypassism." That's our term for using sheer willpower to bypass the deeper mechanisms underlying the stuff that drives your arguments, hurt, and anger. To try to command yourself to stop the negative behavior. Problem is it hardly ever works. And when it does, there's a heavy price: you constrict yourself. It's a desperate attempt to keep the honeymoon alive. Or to look good in others' eyes. Take heart. There is an alternative. That's learning thoroughgoing self-acceptance. Learning to become an Anthetic free spirit. By getting free from all Inner Critic shoulds and condemnation. Once you're free, emotional closeness with your partner will blossom.

 # May 18

We Are Inventors!

Did you know that you are an inventor? You are! When it comes to high-voltage soulmate relationships, it is an act of creation. Of invention. We often see couples who have ended one phase of their relationship—perhaps raising children or building a home or caring for aging parents. It's easy to feel lost or in limbo at such times. That emptiness you feel when you have completed one era in your relationship can be unsettling. Some people think their entire relationship is over. However, if you value each other highly, you'll move into a creative phase. Looking into your natural selves to discover, "What do we want to create together now?" And as you draw on the well of creativity within you, you'll grow together. And reinvent your relationship. There is a well of creative power within you. Let it flow. Renewed love will too.

 # May 19

The Culprit Behind Sexual Blocks

Ever felt sexually blocked? Lack of desire? Shame about your body that blocks your relaxing? Perfectionistic demands you make on yourself to perform? Here's the culprit behind those blocks: Your Inner Critic. It's that part of you (and in all of us) that burdens you with shoulds to perform and criticizes your body and your actions. It blocks your creativity by condemning anything new and interesting you might consider trying. To get free from this inner saboteur, realize that your Inner Critic draws its power from your belief in its messages. You can make a values shift. From valuing living by your Inner Critic's guidance to living from your Natural Self. That's your source of aliveness and creativity. So, take back your rights: I have the right to be fully who I have the capacity to be sexually. I refuse to live by my Inner Critic's commands. Once free, watch your sexual sparks fly!

 # May 20

You Don't Have to Defend Yourself

Are you starring in your own courtroom drama in your intimate relationships? Feel you've committed a crime and have to get acquitted? If all goes well, in the intimate climate of a high-voltage soulmate relationship, your partner will make requests. But it will sound to you like an accusation that you've done something wrong. So, your responses to your partner's requests end up consisting of kneejerk defensive statements. "But I do give you lots of affection." "Why can't you just accept me for who I am?" Such statements are clues that your Inner Critic is pouncing. It's the part of you that's telling you you're guilty. You can put a stop to this whole mechanism with one simple statement: "I don't have to defend myself." It's a message of liberation you speak to yourself. You never have to defend yourself. Instead, get curious. When your partner makes a request, ask, "Can you tell me more about that?"

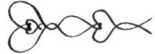 # May 21

To Identify Your Soulmate, You Need to Think Like a Beauty Queen

Ever been told, "You are beautiful," and felt the pull to automatically think, "This must be the one"? It's so heady to be admired, especially if you haven't received a lot of acknowledgement of your beauty, that you can rush into a relationship without checking the person out. But you need to think like a beauty queen. She accepts admiring looks and words of praise, because she's learned that her beauty is a given, so of course, others will see that. She doesn't let that push her into the wrong relationship. Just like her, you need more than one criterion—he thinks I'm beautiful. You need to see if he has other qualities you're looking for in a soulmate. So, enjoy the admiration, and use your Executive Self to see if he meets your other criteria.

 # May 22

You Can Grow from Each Other's Feedback

One of the skills that you'll need in order to have a High-Voltage Soulmate Relationship is Giving and Receiving Feedback. That means lovingly telling each other what you see that might be blocking your optimal relating. For example, "Is your Inner Critic pouncing?" and "Are you in your scared child?" By not just expressing love and approval but also offering perspective about what you see going on with each other, you'll be using your relationship for psychological growth. It's a gift you'd never get being single. Because our partner can see things about us we can't see. Or things that only surface in the context of an intimate relationship. This skill is challenging but, boy, does it reap rich rewards. You'll be closer, and you'll get transformative change.

 # May 23

Here's the Big Block to Your Soulmate Love

Can't seem to find your soulmate? Or think you've found the one but keep sabotaging the closeness you could have? Here's the big block to finding and living out your soulmate love: Your Reactivity. That's the internal structure of thoughts, feelings, and beliefs that you've developed to deal with emotional pain. What emotional pain? The pain caused by your Inner Critic. It's been putting you down for years. Telling you you're defective and inferior. Faced with this load of pain, you had to develop a way to get some relief. So, you started constricting yourself: "Oh, I can't think *that*. I can't say *that*. And I certainly shouldn't feel that." Now, just like a hurt limb that you keep immobile to control the pain, your whole being has become frozen. Constricted. There *is* a way out. Start identifying and challenging your Inner Critic shoulds. "I have the right to think or feel anything. I'm still a good person." As you uncramp your Natural Self; as you let it come alive, you'll be opening yourself to creating your heart's desire. And that means your soulmate love.

 # May 24

Together Forever: How to Do It

"I will love you forever." "Till the end of time." Those words gush forth when our relationships are new. And at first, we try to make love last by being nice. We quickly find, however, that being nice is not enough. High voltage soulmates have as their primary goal, not longevity, but rather optimal relating. That means talking about the relationship; talking about your feelings toward each other; using the relationship for personal growth. It can be done. Jim and I spent our lives developing the relationship skills that will keep you together forever. You won't want to be anywhere else but with your partner. Because once you get a taste of this kind of closeness, the sweet pleasure of it can't be beat anywhere else.

 # May 25

Connecting vs. Withdrawing: We Have a Choice

Sometimes in relationships it feels like we just *have to* withdraw. Maybe in anger. Perhaps in hurt. But once we withdraw, all we get is loneliness. And deeper pain. Oh, sure, there's some initial relief. That's because our anxiety goes down when we withdraw. But, the pain is still there. So, what can you do? *Connect.* Tell your partner through a labeling of your feelings: "I'm feeling angry. I'm feeling hurt. I have an impulse to withdraw." That's going to be the first step in keeping your soulmate love flowing. So, if you're soulmate questing, look for someone who connects by talking to you when they're upset. It's connecting vs. withdrawing. We do have a choice.

 # May 26

Zingers Hurt!

Ever been in a relationship with someone who zings you? By that we mean, when you share something vulnerable with them, like a joy or an area of pain, they can be counted on to put you down, act superior, or criticize you. Sometimes the zingers are so subtle you don't know they're happening. You're just left with an uneasy, troubled feeling. We teach people how to recognize those comments for what they are—acts of contempt and judgmentalism toward you. Zingers are closeness killers. That's why we teach couples to label zingers they deliver with the statement, "That was just my stuff." And then to analyze them for clues to the judgmental partner's Inner Critic. If you love someone, you won't want to zing them. Because zingers hurt.

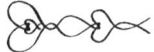 # May 27

How Being Sweet Can Wreck Your Relationship

I saw something about myself that some of you might relate to. I was feeling afraid of a person in my world. Someone who intimidated me. As I talked it over with friends, I realized I'm intimidated because of my own should. The big should I learned as a child—and it haunts me at times today—is to "Be Sweet." Totally Understanding. Compliant. Definitely not expressing anger. Well, that's not good for me. And if you're like me, you know that it's disempowering. Weakening. You end up not just disempowered with the intimidating person but with ordinary tasks you have to do in your life. And you live disempowered with your soulmate. But, as my friends and I talked, I realized I have another option. An option some of you easily deploy. That's to be powerful. Assertive. Even angry. I started cussing. That helped a lot. Now, I'm ready to take on that intimidating person. And to take on life.

 # May 28

How to Never Have a Boring Day in Your Relationship

I've been bored in relationships before. Even came home early from a honeymoon out of boredom. But I never had a boring day in my marriage to Jim. Why? Because he connected. All the time. For example, I'd wake up in the middle of the night to find him not in bed. He'd be sitting on the patio. When I'd cuddle up next to him, he'd say, "Song from yesteryear!" And then he'd sing me an oldies love song. Or he'd say, "I've been thinking about…." These kinds of comments made for an intense connection moment-by-moment. So, I was never lonely and never bored. And, through his example, Jim taught me to do the same. You can do it, too. How? Be forthcoming with your thoughts, your surges of love, your savorings of the relationship, your plans. It's never a boring day in a high-voltage soulmate relationship.

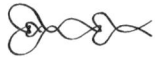 # May 29

Beware of Demonizing

Demonizing. That's seeing your partner as a bad person. Someone with evil intent toward you. You end up holding a grudge against such an awful person. And then you harden your heart. But you know what? No one is a bad person. They're just humans with stuff. Better to ask them to work on their stuff. Get to the root of what's driving their behavior. Then you both can grow. And your relationship will be cared for.

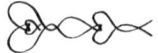 # May 30

Pleasure: It's Important

"Do What Gives You Pleasure Today." That's a guiding value in the Anthetic philosophy of life. Is that hedonistic? Frivolous? Selfish? No! And here's why. When you're doing what gives you pleasure, you're living from your Natural Self—that deep part of you that's full of aliveness. And when you live from your Natural Self, having pleasure as you go, that is good for your mental health. You can't have fun and be depressed at the same time. What's more, when you're happy, you will attract others to you. They'll want to be around you. So, if you're soulmate questing, your pleasure-filled happy spirit will attract your soulmate. And, if you're already in a relationship, your relationship will hum along when you're happy. When you're having pleasure, the love inside you flows. It's a choice. Choose pleasure today. It will be your stepping stone on the path of happily ever after.

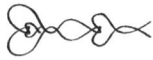 **May 31**

Courage: Here's Where to Find It

Today is a day that's all about courage. It's Memorial Day—the day in the United States where we honor all those who have fought and died in service to our country. We want to stand in honor of these heroes. An interesting thing though: If you ask a hero what led them to act with such courage, they'll more than likely say, "I did it for my buddies," or "I did it for those I love." And those words contain the secret to where courage comes from. It comes from love. So, when it comes to having the courage to be close, look no farther than your own heart. Where your love is, there you will find courage.

June 1

Initiate Reconciliation

Relationship conflict occurs even in the best of relationships. What is needed is the skill of *initiating a reconciliation*. To do so, one partner must actively pursue the other. Pursuing when you've just had conflict and hurt requires valuing three things: closeness, love, and creating a safe haven. It means you resist acting out pain through revenge or distancing. As profound as it is, it's a simple skill that begins with 3 little words, *"Can we talk?"* It will reap a harvest of closeness.

 # June 2

3 Subtle Ways We Deflect Closeness

Teasing. Sarcasm. Humorizing. These are three things people often do in relationships. But they're closeness deflectors. They are defensive maneuvers to derail the intensity of intimacy that's building between you. Each involves making comments that poke fun at or subtly demean the other person. And while the target of such comments may laugh, underneath they'll be experiencing an uneasy feeling of emotional pain. The pain occurs because an opportunity for a soul-satisfying connection just got lost. For a soulmate connection, we need to empathize with the other person. Ask yourself, "Will what I say trigger pain in this person?" Then, "Because I love them, I'm not going to say it."

 # June 3

Let's Debunk Cynicism about Love

Have you heard, "Romantic love just naturally fades;" "Romantic love is an anesthetic that wears off after the honeymoon;" "Soulmates! No such thing;"? These are all cynical comments. What you may not have known is that cynicism is generated by the Inner Critic. It leads you to think that finding and achieving a loving depth connection is idealistic. And predicts that such love is something you could never accomplish. Cynicism needs to be challenged like any other Inner Critic belief. Here are a few challenges to get you started on getting free: "I have the right to be what you call idealistic." "What do you know about love? You're just an Inner Critic; a negative part of me. You don't have a loving bone in your body!" "I choose love. Romantic love. Soulmate love." Now you're on your way!

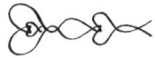 # June 4

Life Pressures Can Lead to Your Soulmate

Have you ever been under extreme pressure in your life? Maybe you are even now. We certainly have. Jim told of how, in his thirties, hardly eking out a living, he thought, "How am I going to make money?" And out of that caldron of not knowing came a breakthrough: "Maybe I should lead groups!" And because he followed that thought, he began to lead groups. And that led to developing Anthetic Therapy. And it thread by thread led to his sitting in a meeting room, waiting to begin his doctoral program, when a young woman sat down next to him. That was me. That was his soulmate. So, take heart. It appears to be a principle: The very life pressures that seem to torment you actually are the force which lead you to make transformative change. And to open the door to your happily ever after. Just follow the next step.

 # June 5

Understanding the Daddy Factor in Relationships

June is Father's Day month. It has me thinking about the "Daddy Factor." That's my term for the almost universal process of looking for a partner who gives us the best of what our dads were to us and subconsciously seeking from our partner the love and emotional connection our dads failed to provide. In one of my early letters to Jim, I told him I was feeling afraid that I was feeling for him was just a longing for "Daddy love." His wise reply: "Why sure. Your feelings to me are Oedipal (Sigmund Freud's term) as are mine toward you. So, what else is new? All we have to do is keep reminding ourselves, 'Jim you are not Daddy. Kathy, you are not Mom.' Let's continue to enjoy our Oedipal feelings. Just not let them drive us to expect perfect parental love from each other." So, soulmate questers, we say to you, the Daddy Factor is normal. Just let your inner Executive Self be in charge of the power you give it in your partner choice and in how you live out your relationship.

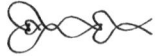 # June 6

Who's Your Daddy Tiger?

"Jim, I claim you as my Daddy Tiger!" Those were words I spoke during our wedding ceremony. As we'd shared our love story with people, we had been bombarded by cynical comments about love. Jim's response had been strong, encouraging words. Words that defended our love and our relationship. That experience of male power uncompromisingly standing for us against the negativity of others was transporting for me. It fulfilled some deep archetypal longing. My prince had come! Perhaps yours has too. If so, let us express our honoring and gratitude to them. If you are soulmate questing, look for a partner who can tap that Daddy Tiger love.

 # June 7

Impulse Control: The Heart of Happily Ever After

Ever thrown a tantrum? Cried when you needed to speak rationally? That's a little child part of you that lacks impulse control. It's a part that feels that others have personal power, but it doesn't. So, it resorts to dramatic emotional outbursts to try to get people to do what it wants. Of course, we pay a price for this. It makes us miserable and creates distance in our relationships. What to do? Say to yourself, "Just because I have an impulse doesn't mean I have to act on it." This will help you disengage from that reactive child part. Then you'll be in shape for the closeness of your happily ever after.

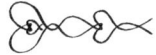 # June 8

Feeling Like a Victim? Here's What to Do

"You won't let me be me." "I feel like I'm being punished." "You won't let me have my feelings." Statements such as these indicate you're feeling like a victim. Although you may feel like blaming someone else for your situation, each of these statements points to your own power giveaway. The one to whom you're giving your power away is your Inner Critic. To take back your power, you'll need to take back your rights to do, be, and feel what your Inner Critic has forbidden. For example, to take back your power when you're thinking, "You won't let me have my feelings," say to your Inner Critic, "I have the right to have my feelings. In fact, all my feelings." As you get free from your Inner Critic, you'll realize you have equal power with your partner (or anyone else). And that's the basis for a good relationship.

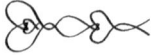 # June 9

You Don't Analyze Too Much!

Has anyone ever told you, "You analyze things too much?" And have you read, "Don't ask 'why' questions?" And did you feel self-doubt; even guilt? Well, we want to say a word of liberation to you: You don't analyze too much! We take the position that people don't ask nearly enough why-questions. When you ask yourself, "Why was I touchy just now?" or "Why was I defensive?" you're taking the step not to function on automatic; instead to live your life in a conscious way. Then when you ask your partner, why-questions, you're actually requesting that they explore any machinery that might be driving their attitudes and behaviors. One more thing: You can then ask why-questions about your relationship. For example, "Why are we fighting so much?" And that will lead to emotional closeness. That's the path to happily ever after.

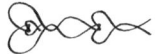 # June 10

You're the Face on My Cake

We threw a Father's Day party for Jim. One of our friends walked in with a big cake box. As she turned it toward us, we could see through the cellophane window. There, baked into the creamy white icing: Jim's and my wedding picture! The words above it read, "Happy Father's Day, Jim." That was a stunning surprise. I'm still savoring it. What an act of love and beholding. Our friend wanted to honor Jim, but she also wanted to celebrate our love. She felt that Jim's specialness and our soulmate relationship was so important, she'd want to bake it on top of the cake. Now it has me thinking to ask you: Who would you honor enough to put their face on a cake? It's an extravagant expression of love. Delicious!

 # June 11

Speak Words of Approval

"I've surveyed your mind, body, and spirit. And over all I see I cast my strong male look of approval." Jim spoke those words to me early in our relationship. They became part of his wedding vows to me. His approval was profound for me. He had come to know me. My history. My flaws. Still he looked at me with approval. It took his living by the values of non-judgmentalism, love, and empathy. Then he drew from a deep spiritual place in himself, and, in effect, blessed me. It was fabulous. You can do this for each other too. Behold one another. Empathize with one another. Speak words of approval today.

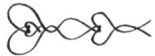 # June 12

Maintain Good Will Toward Your Partner

Giving the benefit of the doubt. Seeing it from their perspective. Softening your heart. All these form an attitude of good will toward your partner. They're in contrast to suspiciousness, demonizing, and hardening your heart. Choosing the latter is a temptation when we're hurting or angry. It is a choice. And what we choose is what we get. Choose good will today. And if you're soulmate questing, choose a partner who values good will as much as you do.

 # June 13

Can You Express Love on Demand?

Have you ever heard, "Don't push me! I can't express love on demand"? That's purely a defensive statement. Its goal is to protect against threats to a sense of independence. Such rigid self-sufficiency leads to distance and loneliness. We support your freedom. But in a new way. Get free from your Inner Critic should first. For example, "I have the right *not* to express love." And, "I have the right *to* express love." Most important, "Just because I express love doesn't mean I have to do anything else." Once free, you can be flexible. You can value closeness. And you can express love on demand. It's a pleasure we don't want you to miss.

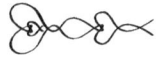 # June 14

Explore the Continent of Your Relationship

"Before us lies the huge continent of our relationship, which we are exploring bit by bit. What a delightful prospect!" Jim wrote this to me only one month after we had met. I love the imagery of it, and wanted to pass it on to you. When it comes to relationships, it can be a wonderful experience of discovery-day after day. To do that, you need to keep revealing yourselves to each other more and more. Here's a simple exploring tool, and it's a reliable one: Ask each other frequently, "What are you feeling?" That is a world all its own. So, we invite you to follow our lead. Be explorers!

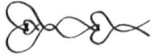 # June 15

Inner Figure Work Will Set You Free

Transformative change. We've said before that it's the gift of high-voltage soulmate relationships. What is transformative change? It's essentially about getting free. That means having psychological distance from any inner figures that cause you pain. For example, a prideful part of yourself that resists feedback; that says, "Nobody's going to change me. I am what I am!" As you step away from such figures and look at their impact on your life, you can then direct what part, if any, you want them to play in your relationship. In this way, you'll no longer be driven by inner figures that sabotage your goal of closeness. You'll be free to create your life in the way that brings you happiness and fulfillment. Now, that's transformative change.

 # June 16

Enfolding Love: Antidote to Fear

It was one month into our long-distance relationship. Jim was facing a fearful moment; something that, in the past, would have been quite intimidating to him. He wrote me these words: "As I faced this, the following thought came to me out of the blue: I am wrapped in the enfolding love of my beloved; there is nothing here to fear." Love is like that. An enfolding blanket that comforts and empowers us. If you're soulmate questing, look for someone whose love has that enfolding quality. Someone who soothes and sources power to you. If you're in a soulmate relationship, feel the comfort and courage available to you. When you face something fearful, you have the antidote.

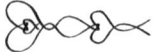 # June 17

You Don't Have to Be Perfect to Find Your Soulmate

You may think, "Once I lose this weight; once I get in shape; once I find the right hair style, then I'll find my soulmate." Don't trust that kind of thinking. We're recommending Anthetic growth—not growth by shaping yourself into the perfect person, but growth that occurs through ever increasing self-acceptance. That includes accepting all the rejected and submerged parts of yourself—parts you submerged because your Inner Critic said they were unacceptable. To do this, you'll need to keep getting free from your Inner Critic's condemnation. Here's a start: Look at how you grouse about your "faults." Then say, "I have the right to have that flaw. I'm still a good person." Then, we recommend you take it a step further and say to yourself, "I bless you, dear fault, and I love you just the way you are." Then, in your soulmate quest, you'll know what words to be listening for. Your soulmate will accept, love, and bless you in your full humanity.

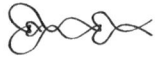 # June 18

The Pursuer-Distancer Crisis Explained

"She wants so much; I feel suffocated." That's the Distancer talking. "I want so little; and I don't even get *that*." That's the Pursuer replying. The more the Pursuer pursues, the more the Distancer distances. The process escalates. Sometimes until it ends in a breakup of the relationship. What's going on? In Anthetic couple work, we discovered the mechanism: The Pursuer's actions are desperate moves toward loving closeness. The Distancer's retreat behind walls is simply a lack of skills needed to be close and still free. What to do? The Pursuer needs to learn to reduce judgmentalism that gets expressed in an attempt to open up the distancing partner. The Distancer needs to learn the Inner Critic challenging skills to be assertive and close. So, if you've found yourself in a Pursuer-Distancer relationship, you can view it as an opportunity for inner freedom. And for growth. And for learning closeness.

 # June 19

Have the Urge to Surrender? You'll Need Flexibility

Surrendering to your beloved. It's an archetypal urge. If you find your soulmate, you'll want to fall into each other. Jim captured it in an early letter to me: "Will you intermingle with me? Will you be closer to me than a sister, closer than a twin, as close as I am to myself? So familiar to each other that anything we say or do would be acceptable." We both felt this way—could not get close enough to each other. Then he touched on the problem in such closeness: "Merging but still being autonomous. Being alter egos for each other—but still separate." Yes, that's the challenge in high-voltage loving. It's what scares many away from it. Take heart, though. It can be done. We've forged the way. Here's the first step: In the face of each other's powerful love, say, "Just because you love me so much doesn't mean I have to do a thing!" You say this as often as you need in order to remain close, yet free. The result: Flexibility. I can surrender to loving you, yet still be me.

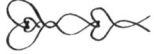 # June 20

The Puppydog Nature of Love

"I feel like a puppydog about going with you to New York, wagging my tail about the chance to be with you on the plane and share experiences at the seminar." Jim wrote that to me when we were living our long-distance relationships those first six months. I loved that he could give me such a vivid picture of how he felt about being with me. When you find your love, that's how you feel. As excited and unashamed as a puppy about showing your love. That attitude is what makes love blossom. If you start being aloof and guarded, you'll just add distance and anxiety to your budding relationship. So, it's a principle of happily ever after: Let your inner puppydog wag!

 # June 21

Am I Pleasing You Enough

"Am I pleasing you enough?" What a wonderful question! It's a question Jim and I asked each other repeatedly during the 22 years of our marriage. We teach the couples who come to us for help to ask this too. It issues from a heart of caring toward your partner. You empathize with their pleasure, so you want them to have as much pleasure as possible. As much as you, their partner, can be the source of. When you and your partner ask each other this question it opens doors to each other's souls. It melts you. You'll say like Jim said to me in his wedding vows: "I want to spend the rest of my life pleasing you."

 # June 22

What to Do if You're Feeling Closed Up

Nobody really wants to feel closed up. It doesn't feel good. Especially in contrast to the ecstatic feelings you've had in the past in your relationship. But we often act in ways that are unwittingly corrosive to closeness. As I read Jim's letter to me from 1989, I saw that he had modeled for us what to do. He wrote. "I must begin by saying I am feeling closed up now; let me see if by writing it I can reconnect with you. Yes, already I am feeling your sweet presence." So, that's how to do it. Two simple steps: First, voice to your partner that you're feeling closed up. Second, state your goal of reconnecting by talking about it. So, to restore closeness, you can rely on the magic of this process.

 # June 23

You Are a Great Mansion to Be Explored

"You are like a great mansion, and you have invited me into you." Jim wrote that two months after we met. What a profound feeling to know he saw me in that way—not just a façade of a person, but some vast personality to come to know. Then he continued, "At first, I stood in the hall while we shyly got to know each other, and then you invited me into an inner room, wondering what my reaction would be. And I loved it, and so now we are exploring this mansion, with you opening one door after another, as you look at my face to see my reaction. And I love this house of you, and we are wondering whether to open the door to the bedroom…" I loved this metaphor. We're offering it to you, soulmate quester. That's the attitude your soulmate will have—wanting to know you deeply, all your facets, nooks, and crannies. We're offering it to you, soulmates, as encouragement to go deeper with each other. It's heart-pounding romance. It will take a lifetime to discover the mansion that is your beloved.

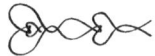 # June 24

How to Recognize Your Soulmate: 3 Guiding Principles

How will you recognize your soulmate? It's easy to let your heart run ahead of you. It's full of hope and love. But you'll need clear thinking. Jim's letter to me two months after we met offers three principles by which you can be guided. He wrote: "Here's a list of things I *treasure* about you, things I *value* you for, things you give that are such that I *would never leave you*." Then he went on to enumerate 13 qualities I had. Perhaps hearing some of them will help you with your list. They included my spirituality; that I was in the same field of work as he; that I was willing to work on stuff; that I took the initiative. The message we can take from Jim's principles is that your soulmate will have specific traits, identifiable by you as very highly valuable. Not someone you're lukewarm about. Your soulmate will be your treasure.

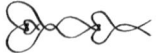 # June 25

Bedtime Stories: Communication Enhancer

Bedtime stories. It was a childhood pleasure for many of us. A one-on-one time of connection with our parent or caregiver. There's something in this cherished ritual for us to use in enhancing our adult intimate relationship. We've been thinking about what made it so special and have identified 3 ingredients: 1) Focused verbal communication from your loved one to you; 2) content that captivates your interest; 3) feedback about what you liked and didn't like in the story. Jim and I had car seminars, couch seminars, and patio seminars throughout our marriage—Jim choosing an article from magazines or books and reading them to me. Then our discussing them, critiquing them, sharing what we liked about them. It's a great pleasure. Try it. Mealtime, after-work, bedtime. There was something heart-fulfilling about those bedtime stories. Make them part of your relationship. Your communication will deepen. Closeness will grow.

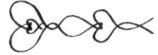 # June 26

It's Okay to Ask for Reassurance

Is it okay to ask for reassurance when you're in a relationship? Short answer: Absolutely! If you want emotional closeness, you need to state your need for reassurance, and your partner needs to respond. Here's how Jim spoke about it in his letter to me: "As far as I'm concerned it is ALWAYS okay to ask for reassurance at any time. I am willing to go a very long way to safeguard our relationship's depth, to brace it with tactical measures that give it a supportive context within which it can flourish." And there you have it. When you've found your soulmate, you want to protect and support that relationship. Giving reassurance is essential.

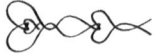 # June 27

3 Essential Qualities of Strength

Does strength mean being aggressive and dominating? No. "Strength is being able to confront conflict and deep feelings; listening to the other's pain; not abandoning the one you love when the going gets rough." That's how Jim explained it to me in an early letter. When you are soulmate questing, look for someone who exhibits this strength. It will show as you share your feelings. If you're living a soulmate relationship keep growing in strength as you confront the intensities of feeling your partner exhibits. As I said in my wedding vows, "Stand with the pain until you get through to the other side."

 # June 28

Don't Say "What's the Matter"

Everybody says it: "What's the matter?" We're attuned to each other. We see the other's distress. We mean well when we ask. The problem with this form of inquiring is that it is unskilled. It's ineffective. It most often triggers a defensive response. Here's a better question: "What are you feeling?" Use these exact words. If you ask, "*How* are you feeling," you'll get the conventional response, "Fine." The word *what* is key. It calls us to think. "Hmm. What *am* I feeling?" This skill is golden. Use it often.

 # June 29

Soulmates Don't Give Each Other the Cold Shoulder

The cold shoulder. It means deliberately being cold and unsympathetic. It's chilling to even think of it. It happens when one partner doesn't value the other or is so blocked by anger or fear, they're driven to be uncaring. Jim wrote me early on, "In other relationships, I asked for things I ask you, and I got the cold shoulder." My valuing of Jim was so huge and my love was so profound that I never thought of not responding to or rejecting him. And that's how soulmate love feels. When you find your soulmate, you won't get the cold shoulder. You'll get the warmth of open arms.

 # June 30

When You're Doubting the Goodness of Your Life

I just discovered this thought tucked away in a binder. It's something Jim said to me on a day when I was discouraged. I want to share it with you: "When you're doubting the goodness and purpose of your life, because of sickness or other challenges, remember: Your life has been a flow of your own efforts at fulfilling your natural Self, plus miraculous interventions by the Universe. My life is being watched over and guided by a powerful benevolent force who opens windows of opportunity at amazing times. There is Divine Order, and I am in it." We hope this encourages and comforts you, as it does me.

July 1

Soulmates Are Risk-Takers

"Can I really be close to him? Can I trust him? Can I really call him? Dare I ask him for things?" Those are questions I asked myself about Jim, then dived in and followed through on each one. Jim wrote in the first month of our meeting: "I want us to take even more risks—say things about which we might think, "Oh, I couldn't say that!' Risk making mistakes. Risk triggering stuff in the other person (because we're willing to work on it if it comes up.)" How can soulmates do this? By a commitment to talk about their feelings. Jim continued, "Now, if you ever feel uncomfortable with anything I say or write, I want you to tell me. I'd like an agreement from you that you will tell me of any negative reactions you have. Okay?" So, I did. And, because I risked, and he risked, and we talked about our feelings, we got more and more closeness. And you will too.

 # July 2

What to Do if You're at a Loss for Words

Ever been at a loss for words? It's a pivotal moment in an intimate relationship. You can freeze up. That will produce distance. Or you can put your loss for words into words! Listen to what Jim did in his early letter to me: "I am at a loss for words. I love you so much, I can hardly stand it." With that report of his feelings, I felt close to him. So, here's another skill for creating high-voltage closeness: Speak what you're feeling. Even if it's that you're inarticulate. When you do that, your partner will have a window into your inner world. You will be heart-connected.

July 3

"Nothing in the World Is Single"

"Nothing in the world is single," writes Shelley. "All things by a law divine in one spirit meet and mingle." Jim quoted Shelley's poem to me in July, 1989, our wedding month. He was meditating that an archetype of unification was driving us to merge, yet still retain our identities. It's an experience you will likely have. It draws us out of ourselves and toward each other. Here's more of Shelley's beautiful poem to bless your day: "The mountains kiss the heavens. The waves clasp one another. The sunlight clasps the earth. The moonbeams kiss the sea."

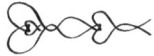 # July 4

Glitchwork Gives Us Power

Glitches can have a curious benefit to soulmate partners. A glitch is a strained communication, even an argument, over stuff either partner is having. You'd think it would harm the relationship. And, of course, if left unprocessed, it certainly can. But, Jim and I discovered the gift that a glitch can contain—power. Jim wrote it this way: "Our glitchwork gives us, ultimately, more power. Power to confront a negative feeling in the other. Power to trust. Power to soothe our little inner child parts, as they feel scared by the high voltages of our relationship." We were using the skills Jim had developed with his groups. And they were serving us well. Skills like asking each other, "What are you feeling?" and "Can you tell me more about that?" Try them. And watch your love and power grow.

 # July 5

Has the Question Mark Left Your Partner's Voice?

Questioning. It comes with the territory of the early part of your relationship. Will she accept me for all that I am? Will he go away? Jim and I had all those wonderings too. We were getting to know each other. Risking to reveal more and more about ourselves. Jim even wrote me an entire letter with his "flaws." I wrote to him of my insecurities—would he go away once we began a sexual relationship? For both of us, we were answering the question, "Have we really found our soulmate?" It didn't take long to find our answer. I just found (in an old purse from 1989) a note I had written on a scrap of paper. It reads, "The question mark has left his voice." His words, his tone, his attitude all said, "You're the one. I'll never leave you." So, if you're soulmate questing, listen for it. Has the question mark left his voice?

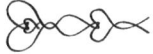 # July 6

Protect Your Relationship

Have you noticed that not everyone supports your relationship? Some want to chew it up. That was Jim's and my experience before we got married. We had to stand strong and defend our relationship against those who were critical of either of us or of marriage in general. We had to realize that some people have hardened their hearts against love. In the face of their attitude and comments, you have to tap your inner strength. Stand for your beloved and your relationship. Protect each other.

 # July 7

Not Perfect? You Need Retrieval Skills

Once you find your soulmate, you may want it to be perfect. But, of course, you aren't perfect. We want to assure you. You don't need perfection. You just need *retrieval skills*. Those are skills for when you make a mistake in relating. The mistakes you make may seem devastating to you. They did to me. But Jim taught me two things for such moments: 1) All feeling devastated means is that your Inner Critic is pouncing. 2) Mistakes simply require course corrections. You can retrieve any situation that has gone astray. One thing you can say is, "That was just my stuff. And I want to process it." With a determination to immediately correct your mistake and the skills to set it right, you can keep your high-voltage relationship humming along.

 **July 8**

Are You Suffering from "Why Attacks"?

"Why didn't I keep my mouth shut?" "I don't know why I'm so emotional." Have you found yourself saying things like this? In Anthetic Therapy, we call such statements, "Why Attacks." While they may seem natural and normal, they actually are clues that your Inner Critic is pouncing. That inner torturer is delivering messages that you should keep your mouth shut; that you should not be emotional. We have some liberating news for you: From here on out, you never again have to believe the propaganda of your Inner Critic that you must constrict yourself. You've now got your Inner Critic's number. "Why Attacks" are pure Inner Critic stuff. Today, you can get free from every one of them by saying, "I have the right *not* to keep my mouth shut. I have the right to open it wide!" and "I have the right to be emotional."

July 9

Get Free from "Who Attacks"

"Who do I think I am to be looking for a soulmate?" When you say, "Who do I think I am," that's what we call a "Who Attack." It comes directly from your Inner Critic, supposedly trying to "protect" you by pressuring you to lower your expectations, keep a low profile, and not do any risky things. Our message; in fact, our mission is to empower you to get free. Free to imagine great things for your life; deep fulfillment in your relationships; and yes, a soulmate! Start getting free now by challenging your Inner Critic: "I have the right to look for a soulmate." "I have the right to have great expectations for my life." Inner freedom is yours for the claiming.

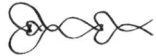 # July 10

Talk about Your Relationship

There's you, me, and our relationship. Couples often talk about the "you" part and the "me" part. But they omit talking about the "relationship." And that's an omission that will deprive you of the intense level of closeness that's possible. When you talk about your relationship, you get to step back and behold what the two of you have created as a bond. You savor its wonder. You assess its deficiencies. You make plans for improving it. Try this today: "What I love about our relationship is…." And "What I'd like us to do different about our relationship is…." You'll see. You'll benefit by realizing there's a third party created by the two of you. It has a life of its own.

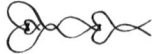 # July 11

Labeling: A Skill for Closeness

"I'm thinking." "What I'm about to say feels scary." "This is shameful for me, but I'm going to share it anyway." That's called *labeling*. It's a wonderful communication skill for producing closeness. It gives your partner a glimpse into your inner world. The secret to its power is that you're not just offering your partner silence. You're not merely offering the pure content of your spoken words. You're instead stepping back from yourself, noting to yourself what's happening inside you, then sharing it. That will produce connection. And a high-voltage relationship.

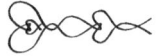 # July 12

Are You Rigidly Dependent?

This is a hard one for me to write about. It's something I struggle in getting free from. I want to share it with you, in case you struggle with this too or have a partner who does. I'm referring to rigid dependency. That's captured so beautifully in one line from an old song about "Sweet Alice," "who wept with delight when you gave her a smile and trembled with fear at your frown." We who identify with Sweet Alice live in a hypervigilant state about possible rejection and abandonment. We tend to idealize others; see ourselves as less than. What gets us angry (although we have a hard time admitting it) is if others refuse to give us the supplies of love and approval we crave. The good news is We Can Be Free of this hyper-dependency. What it takes is understanding that the Inner Critic is the source of our feelings of inferiority and thus dependency. To challenge this mistaken belief, we need to create a welcoming place for our own feelings of anger and for exercising independence. We can use this Anthetic mantra: "I'm all I've got, and that's enough." I know today and pass on to you that my worth as a person is a given. I accept every part of who I am—dependent and self-sufficient. When we do this, we embrace all of who we are.

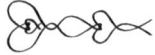 # July 13

One Vital Way to Recognize Your Soulmate

"I want to say flatly that I want as much of you as I can possibly get." Jim wrote that one month after we met. Then he added, "Having said that, I am willing to enjoy whatever parts of your life that you are willing to share with me. Your love. Your fine mind. Your tenderness and sensitivity. Your spirituality. And all the other things about you I cherish. They are so precious to me." I'm sharing this with you as a beacon; a standard by which you may guide your soulmate quest. When you find your high-voltage soulmate, they will want as much of you as they can get. If the person isn't hungry for you, they're not valuing you enough to be the one. Keep looking!

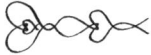 # July 14

How to Understand Touchiness

If you feel touchy and defensive, it's not a crime. It's simply your fear that some disowned part of yourself will be discovered. If you wish to take the path of personal growth, you can use this touchiness as an opportunity to allow that submerged part to come to your consciousness. I had this experience on a trip Jim and I took some years back. I told Jim, "I'm being touchy. And now I know what it's about. I'm wanting my touchiness to intimidate you into stopping talking. And I see that the whole purpose is so you won't trigger my Inner Critic and its condemnation of me!" It was a fabulous eureka moment. Not only did I get free from my Inner Critic, but I also connected with Jim at a deep level—the level of revealing my hidden psyche. As you learn and practice the skills for getting free from your Inner Critic, you'll receive these two gifts: inner freedom and a high-voltage soulmate relationship with your partner.

July 15

Do You Have Trouble Losing?

Do you have to get ahead of other cars on the road? If someone tells you they just bought a new phone, do you have to talk about *your* phone and how much better it is? Do you hate excuses? Hate to be conned? Is your motto, "I don't take shit from no one"? If these statements describe you, you most probably have developed rigid Toughness as a way to deal with anxiety and pain. Yes, it works to armor you against pain. But, you've probably found that it doesn't work in relationships. It destroys closeness and even the relationship itself. That's because at those critical moments of conflict and pain with your partner, you choose winning instead of reconciling; hardening your heart instead of softening; getting revenge instead of closeness. What's the solution? Realize that it's your Inner Critic that has commanded Toughness and criticizes you for any tenderness you display. Then, challenge your Inner Critic should with, "I have the right to lose, to soften, to choose closeness." It's a radical value shift that will transform you. It will permit you to add Tenderness to your repertoire. You'll have the success you seek—but this time in relationships.

 **July 16**

The Switch: You Need to Understand It

The Switch: They begin the relationship being close and loving. But at some point, they'll feel smothered. Begin to start arguments over petty things. Say, "I need my space" and "I don't want to talk about it." It's puzzling to both the Switcher and their partner. Why does the switch from closeness to distance happen? Because the Switcher lacks the ability to be assertive on a day-to-day basis. So, in intimate relationship, they'll inevitably end up feeling suffocated and trapped. To the Switcher, it looks like the cause of those suffocating feelings is his partner or the marriage. Actually, it's his Inner Critic—constricting him from saying what he wants and needs in the relationship without having to work up enough anger to justify it. Bottom line is the Switcher just wants to feel free. We help Switchers get truly free. By challenging those Inner Critic should to not rock the boat, to not ask for what they want. Once free from the Inner Critic, our tolerance for closeness increases. In fact, it's the only way to enjoy it.

 # July 17

Do You Have to Be Perfect to be Soulmates?

Ah, the impulse to be perfect! It's always with us. So, of course, it will tug at us when we find our soulmate. Only two months after Jim and I met, he set us on the right path. I want to share with you what he wrote: "Let us continue to help each other, with patience and love, with the ability to accept any mistakes either of us might make; remember that any such mistake is always correctable. We don't have to do this perfectly; all we have to do is learn as we go." You don't have to be perfect. Just be a learner.

 # July 18

Your Identity: Do You Have to Give It Up for Your Soulmate?

Oh, it's a temptation: To twist yourself into a pretzel for your soulmate. To give up your identity so you won't displease them. So, they won't leave. I've felt that too. Here's how Jim guided me about this in his early letter: "I need you to be free, creative, your own person, mentally powerful, able to challenge me. I need a full human being. I care about you so much that I want you as you are, not a pretzelized Kathyoid. I will not leave you just because you continue to be yourself. I will go on being charmed and pleased by your otherness." There you have the map. Dare to be yourself. Your soulmate will behold your otherness. And will let the wonder of it sink in.

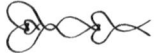 # July 19

Want to Know if You're Loved?

Want to know whether you're loved or liked? Feel embarrassed to ask? It's just not done, right? Wrong! High-voltage partners do it all the time. In fact, it's necessary. "Do you love me?" or "Do you like me?" are more than requests for information. They're requests for the *expression* of warm feelings. If your partner is not interested in expressing such feelings, she or he is not interested in having a high-voltage relationship of intense closeness. If your partner says "Yes," here's the next question to ask, "What do you love about me?" The love that gets expressed fans the flame of your soulmate connection. It can warm a heart, a home, a life.

 # July 20

Don't Miss Your Animus Blessing!

You are being blessed all the time! When that stranger opens the door for you; when your partner brings you coffee in bed; when your neighbor asks if you need help; when your mentor teaches you how to actualize your capabilities. I've given these a name: *animus blessing*. The animus blessing occurs when a man offers a woman words or actions marked by those archetypal energies of strength, protection, clarity of understanding, empowerment, and tenderness. As little girls, we're "daddy's little princess"; as teens in our prom dress, he says, "You'll be the belle of the ball"; as a young adult, he accompanies us in our search for a college to attend. Having received such blessings all her life or never having gotten them, a woman longs unconsciously to receive them from her partner. They are happening all the time. Today, don't miss your animus blessing!

July 21

Do You Want More Closeness?

Do you want more closeness but keep coming up lacking? You know the longing for a deeper connection? We wanted that too. Here's what you need: *Involvement Skills.* There are 3 main ingredients of involved conversations: 1) You're truly interested in what your partner says; 2) you take what they say seriously; and 3) you come to grips with it. Now, that will require your being interested in your partner and empathizing with your partner. The opposite of involvement is silence or monosyllable answers. To experience involvement, ask Interested Questions and give Fully Responsive Answers. Read our love letters. They're full of involvement. As you experience your own involved conversations, you'll feel the thrill of closeness. That's high-voltage relating.

 **July 22**

Step Back from Yourselves! Behold!

We can live only in the experience. Well, that's nice. Or we can deepen our ecstasy by stepping back from ourselves and beholding who we are as a couple. This is how Jim did it in his early letter to me: "I want to tell you how pleased I am at the way we bring up issues and glitches and process them immediately…how well we function together. We move very fast, darling, and we dig very deep. As we work through issue after issue, I feel more and more bonded." As he wrote those words, and as I read them, our closeness intensified. When you step back and observe yourselves, you'll have the opportunity to evaluate how you're doing, then to tweak any spots that you'd like, then to celebrate what you are creating. You'll create bliss.

 # July 23

You Can Be Each Other's Midwives in Growth

"Yes, you are indeed in labor, giving birth—and to what you do not know, nor do I—but I will be here to give you whatever help you wish and to hold your dear hand when it gets painful, and encourage you to bear down. I am here (as with my therapy clients) to help you give birth to yourself." Jim wrote that to me only one month into our relationship. I was in an intense change and growth process. And that can be painful, as you may know. It was incredibly comforting to have Jim beside me (psychologically speaking; he was 2000 miles away). His support and encouragement helped me birth strength and clarity and self-expansion. And happiness. Just as Jim was for me, you can be each other's midwives in your own growth processes. Just listen, encourage, and stand with the other in their pain, holding them. It will be a wondrous experience.

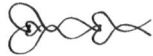 # July 24

You're Vulnerable; You Need a Tender Response

If you have a soulmate heart, you risk being vulnerable in relationships. So, it's vital that your partner treat your vulnerability with tenderness. Jim addressed this in his early letter to me: "I feel so honored that you are trusting to put in my care the tender, precious parts of yourself. I know what it means, and the importance of it. I am so glad that I can welcome them and know them for the precious treasures that they are, and cherish them. You can say or write ANYTHING to me, the most vulnerable and scary things, and I will receive them with awe and love and perfect acceptance." In the unconditional love that he gave me, I went deeper into revealing myself. And we crafted our high-voltage relationship. As you are soulmate questing, be listening for an attitude like Jim's in your partner. It's the attitude you'll both need for intense closeness.

 # July 25

You Can't Stop Talking about Your Love

"Mama, I think I'm in love." That's what I told my mother just a month into knowing Jim. It was a big deal for me to make that announcement to her, because I had learned from teen years to have shame about loving. That didn't matter anymore. I was bursting with the news that I had found my soulmate. Jim, too, couldn't contain his excitement: "I tell everyone about you—my dentist yesterday; a colleague." When you find your soulmate love, you'll want to share it with everybody. That love is so powerful it overcomes normal social reticence and even old psychological pain. You won't be able to stop talking about your love.

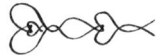 # July 26

When You're Upset, Where Do You Turn?

I'm recalling one day when I got upset. It was a day packed with stresses. I needed soothing and support. I knew where to turn. I talked to my soulmate. Jim wasn't feeling well, but I said, "Sweetheart, I'm troubled." And I dived in. I confided in him and asked him for guidance. He, even though weak from illness, nodded or shook his head to guide me in the things I told him I was considering doing. Then I asked him, "Is my sharing this with you upsetting to you?" He shook his head, "No." That's how soulmates are. When they're upset, they turn to each other. It's what keeps you close.

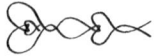 # July 27

You Are My Refuge and My Comfort

Ugh! I should not have eaten those spicy shrimp. They made me sick. It wasn't the first time I'd felt ill in our marriage. Each time, Jim was true to his promise that he would attend to my slightest qualm. Even as he became bedridden by a severe stroke, he remained there for me. I rested my head on his shoulder and told him how I felt. He took my hand in his and held it tightly. I felt his incredible strength and succorance toward me. It is a great gift not to have to be self-sufficient in the face of physical challenges. Soulmates say, "You are my refuge and my comfort."

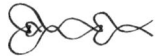 # July 28

Silence: It's Not Golden

"Silence is golden." It's one of those sayings you have to critique. What's wrong with it? It's a way that partners act out their emotional pain. It's often a way of evading making a response that would feel humiliating. It's a way of ignoring your partner. At some level, it's meant to hurt. This all adds up to that it's disrespectful. And it's uncaring. So, beware of silence. It will kill closeness. Instead, report the pull to be silent. Say, "I have a pull to be silent, but I'm not going to go there." Instead, talk about your pain. For example, "I'm feeling hurt. I have a request. There's something I want from you." In other words, keep talking to each other. But from your vulnerability. It will maintain closeness. It will keep your love alive. And it will feel a lot better.

 # July 29

How to Handle Your Partner's Insecurity

It's bound to happen. Somewhere along the path of your relationship, your partner will feel some insecurity. It might be externally triggered—like by a flirtatious other. Or it might be internally generated—like by an old hurt that resurfaces. You might feel puzzled how to handle it. Jim knew just what to do: Effusive Reassurance. Here are his words to me in his early letter: "I sensed your insecurity during our telephone conversation this morning. I want to tell you in no uncertain terms, without any equivocation whatever. I want only you. No other woman. Ever. You are woman enough for me. There's no need for anything else." That fabulous man assured me two fundamental things that set my mind to rest: 1) He held the value of exclusiveness in our relationship. And he had a good reason—he wanted to vouchsafe we'd have as much closeness as possible. 2) He valued me above all others. I was it. So, those elements are what you'll need to include in your response to your partner's insecurity. They're powerfully reassuring.

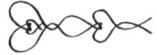 # July 30

God Is Intertwined with Us

Where is God in soulmate love? We pondered this as our love grew and developed. Jim wrote his thoughts to me: "Surely God flows through us. We express God to each other. He is intertwined with us? He energizes our sexual experiences and praises our boldness? He unfolds in us; yes. We have to let him into our lives. He shares in our joys, both sexual and other. He is quite intimate with us." Jim's groping words captured that we didn't receive this as dogma. We were experiencing this: that a benevolent God was with us. God was in the thick of it with us. Observe your own soulmate journey. See if God isn't in it with you.

 # July 31

Procrastinating? Here's the Secret to Why

If you're a procrastinator, you're in good company. Many, many people are. Even if it's only an occasional problem for you, it's one that's almost universal at one time or other in people's lives. Puzzled? Here's the secret: It's your Inner Critic. When your Inner Critic is strong, procrastinating may be the only way you can resist its pressure. One more thing: you may be thinking you *should* do this thing you're avoiding, but deep inside, your Natural Self does not want to do it at all. Yet, your Inner Critic has you in its grip, so that you can't attend to what your Natural Self is telling you. To become clear about which is the case, first challenge your Inner Critic, "I have the right not to do this! I'm still a good person." Once free, you will feel either the relief of being set free from a burdensome task or you will feel fresh sparks of energy for the task from your Natural Self.

August 1

A Test for Happily Ever After Love

"Come on full blast, girl. You will never overwhelm me with wanting to be with me. For I want to be with you as much as you want to be with me." Jim wrote that to me just one month after we met. We want to encourage you with these words. You may have been with a partner who didn't want as much closeness as you do; who said, "Back off" rather than "Bring it on." That's a clear sign that you're with someone who is a voltage mismatch for you. If you want high-voltage connection; that is, a lot of emotional closeness and sharing the full power of your inner selves, here's the test: If you indicate that you want a lot of closeness, they'll respond like Jim did: "My heart's desire is the same as yours. I want to be together as much as possible." They might even add, as Jim did, "I welcome being overwhelmed by your sweet presence."

 # August 2

Do You Have Trouble Making Decisions?

"I just can't decide." Ever said that? Most of us do at some time or other. Whether it's choosing what restaurant to eat at or whether to marry someone, it's not uncommon to think, "No matter what I decide it's going to be the wrong thing." We've discovered what such indecision is about. It's that you're out of touch with your Natural Self. That's the part of you that's full of aliveness and knows what it wants. The reason you can't access your Natural Self: You've bought into your Inner Critic should. Once you do that, your Natural Self wishes get obscured. What to do? Get free from your Inner Critic. Identify each should that's blocking your decision-making. Then declare a releasing statement. You have the right to make decisions that lead to a happy life. We support you in going for your bliss.

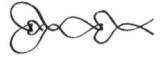 # August 3

The Quantum Leap: Finding Your Soulmate

"Our meeting is having a profound effect on us. We have, it seems, taken a quantum leap into a new way of being. It was just a sort of orientation session, and all we did was talk about our deepest concerns and then shared our love, but the ripples from that are still spreading through our lives; it was a big bang emotionally speaking." I'm quoting Jim's letter to me one month after our first meeting. That meeting was a perfect example of what is called a peak experience, in which a person's sense of who they are and their place in the universe is fundamentally shifted. Like us, when you find your soulmate, it will be a peak experience. In fact, it will be a quantum leap in your life.

 # August 4

Should You Search for a Soulmate?

Are we convinced that you should *search* for a soulmate? Or should you wait passively for one to appear? Jim chronicled his active search for me this way: "I began my search for you in 1941, in Detroit, little knowing that you hadn't been born yet. Let's skip to November, 1951, the first time there was a possibility of finding you. In that month, I was back in the Navy in Pensacola, still searching. You weren't there." His letter follows his journey to California in the 1960s; to his master's program in 1985; then finally to his doctoral program in 1989: "By now I had a list of criteria. And then there you were, sitting next to me in Curlew, our meeting room. The more I found out about you, the more I realized it was you! And so, I began to fall in love with you." As for me, I had given up on ever finding a soulmate. Yet, as I walked into that meeting room, some locked-away part of me; the soulmate part, came alive. She saw Jim and sat in the chair next to him. She had found her man. As we step back from our individual stories to share with you, here's what we see: We were both actively pursuing our dream—getting our doctorate. And we each had a longing for a soulmate that could not be quelled. So, there's no stopping it. Whether or not your mind will admit, your heart will be searching.

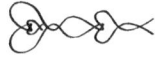 # August 5

Are You Afraid to Be Happy?

"I am so happy. But I feel uneasy. Like something's going to get me for it." That feeling had emerged as he got freer and freer in therapy. He had begun to live from his Natural Self, following his sparks. Now, he had a new problem—anxiety about being happy. What is that? It's a fear of being punished for having pleasure. It has its roots in early learning. Perhaps from a parent, a teacher, a religious institution. If you've developed that fear, Anthetic challenging will help you get released from it. We recommend you claim, "I have the right to be happy. My life is in my hands now. No one can punish me anymore. I have the power to no longer have contact with people who don't support my happiness." We wish you deep happiness today.

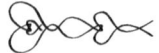 # August 6

Use Your History to Recognize Your Soulmate

Dear Soulmate Quester, here is our gem for you today. It's guidance on how to recognize your soulmate. You've got it right in your memory bank. What we're suggesting is that you do a mental survey of your past partners. We know. Retrieving memories of your relationship history may seem like opening a Pandora's box of pain. However, it's actually a treasure chest of valuable information on what to look for in a life partner. Here's what to do: List each partner's name. Then write a column titled, "What I got from this person that I loved." Then write another column titled, "What I didn't get from them that I want." Finally, "What I got from them that caused me pain." From these lists you can extract the qualities you're looking for in a soulmate. The insights you gain will clear your vision. With clear eyes, you'll recognize your soulmate.

 # August 7

Do You Want to Make Your Relationship Solid?

"Our marriage becomes more and more solid: first the comforter, now we have a telephone number!" Jim was writing to me one month before our wedding. He was talking about our desire to take this love we had; an invisible thing made of heart and spirit, and make it solid and visible. We wanted to manifest our love so we could see it and touch it. In fact, so anyone could see it. So, our first big purchase together was our comforter. It was a scary purchase—hundreds of dollars, at a time when we didn't have much money. But there it was at the department store, in all its effusively beautiful glory. We decided our marriage bed was such an important item that we would splurge and buy something that would represent its worth to us. Then, I got our telephone installed in our patio home where we would live. More solidity. More proof of our love and our intention to bond. As you are deciding whether someone is your soulmate, look for this clue. Are you buying items together that symbolize your love? Do you both long to make your relationship solid?

 # August 8

Don't Micromanage Your Relationship

"Did you put out the trash yet?" "Are you making sure our hotel room has a microwave?" "Be sure to tell your haircutter not to cut your hair so short this time." All are examples of micromanagement. To define the term, it's when you make lists of things for your partner to do, then carefully monitor every project done to make sure it's being done exactly the way you would do it. It's a form of coercive control. I know about this. I'm a recovering micromanager. Jim helped me with this one. I had no idea what I was doing. I just knew I felt anxiety when he was in charge of getting something done, and I wasn't. The antidote? I learned to value being easygoing. As Jim said, not to get shook up. To make this shift requires feedback from your partner. If you'd like to do this, ask your partner, "Please tell me every time you see me doing something that's controlling." Jim's way was to say to me, "I have a request that you not over-monitor me." You can change this. You'll be working toward having a more mutual relationship. And you'll be more relaxed.

 # August 9

Your Inner World: Monsters Inside?

Sometimes it can feel scary to get in touch with your feelings. We tend to be reluctant to disturb the fragile truce we've achieved with our Inner Critic. We've managed to keep the pain the Inner Critic delivers at bay by locking away whole chunks of our inner world. It might be tender feelings that are stuffed down. Or maybe assertive feelings. Or sometimes even our hopes and dreams. We get to the point where we don't want to explore our inner world. We're afraid we'll discover monsters inside. We want to assure you that any inner material that seems like monsters is only because the Inner Critic calls it that. In reality, they are beautiful, playful, cuddly puppies over which a spell has been cast to make them look like monsters. As you bit by bit begin to explore your feelings, your wonderfulness will begin to emerge. You'll bring that wonderful person you are into your outer world to bless all of us.

 # August 10

Do You Like to Start Fights with Your Partner?

"I don't like it when you're oppositional." Jim's words to me. "When I say something, you automatically oppose it." Ooh, I don't want to be that way. I ask him, "What is that about?" "You want to start a fight," he says. Hmm. Let me get curious. "Is it a buffer? Something that props up my self-esteem? If I allowed myself to agree with you or be influenced by you, I'd feel one-down?" He's nodding. "Yes." Okay. I'm going to monitor myself about that. Just because I agree with Jim or am influenced by him doesn't make me less of a person. There. I just got a bit freer. That feels better.

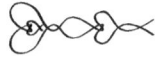 # August 11

You Are My Guru

I was reading Elizabeth Gilbert's book, *Eat, Pray, Love* to Jim. She said a guru is a person who has achieved a state of poise, able to step back from whatever is happening and be even-minded, even blissful. A Guru is one other thing: someone who can pass that state on to others. I said to Jim, "That's you! Even with your stroke and its impact on your body, you have that poise, that bliss." He nodded. "Yes." I asked, "Is it because you disengage from troubles." He: "Yes." Me: 'Yet you can merge fully with me and others." He: "Yes." Me: "I see that in you. You teach me. You are my Guru." He: "Yes." Me: "Have I also been yours?" He: "Yes." Our experience suggests to us that each of us can grow to a place where we can be each other's Guru. As we practice disengaging from worries, internal reactivity, drivenness, we become an example to others. We can then pass it on.

 # August 12

A Toddler's Word Could Save Your Relationship

One of the first words you probably spoke as a toddler was, "Ouch." It's such an effectively expressive word, you'll probably continue using it into old age. Of course, you know that it's the most workaday ready-to-hand word to express your pain when you stub your toe or cut your finger. What you may not know is that word has a use that could save your marriage. How? It's absolutely the simplest way to express your emotional pain when your partner zings you with an angry or judgmental comment. We've found that it brings your partner up short; lets them know you're in pain at what they've said. Once you've said it, you don't have to say anything to retaliate. And that's why it can save your relationship. It stops the cycle of negativity that can erode love and closeness. Try it. It's a little word, but it's powerful.

 # August 13

Are You an Approval Addict?

Eigenlich. German philosopher Martin Heidegger coined this term. It means becoming your own self. No longer living from a herd-mentality. No longer machinelike doing what others expect of you. Instead it's engaging in that amazing process of progressively and increasingly accessing the potentials that exist in your psyche. Then freely deploying any of those potentials as you choose to. It's also called individuation. It is a process. As it continues you are no longer trapped by a driven overconcern with what other people think about you. You are less and less addicted to their approval. You may still enjoy approval, but you no longer are driven by such a strong craving for it. You define yourself as a separate entity. You disengage more and more from the should imposed by your Inner Critic. Yes, you are a free spirit.

 # August 14

Reach Out to Each Other

If you want to connect; to break free from pride-and-fear-induced isolation, you need to Reach Out. A reach-out occurs when you initiate a Conversation; ask an Interested Question; Express Positive Feelings; and Initiate a Reconciliation. You can also offer to shake hands; touch your partner's shoulder or arm; ask, "Can we talk about such-and-such?"; ask a small group at a gathering, "Mind if I join you?'" and ask someone for help. Reaching out can be scary. It makes you vulnerable to rejection. To overcome your fear of reaching out, you can make such releasing statements as: "I have the right to reach out to this person" or "If I'm rejected, it won't be the end of the world, and they'll be missing out on a good person; namely, me."

 # August 15

How Love Can Go Wrong

Most people think they know how to love. The truth is, however, that much of the time they are doing reactive love. That is love that's given as a kind of commodity that requires a return. Or love that is possessive and controlling. Or love that demands that the other person surrender identity and autonomy. We want to propose the concept of Anthetic love. That is love that consists of warm feelings that you express simply because it feels good to you, whether you get love back or not. Now, to do this kind of love, you'll need to unblock the love that is inside you. As you learn to get free from your Inner Critic and other reactive parts that drive you, your love will flow freely. It's soul-fulfilling.

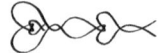 # August 16

The Problem with Dating Games

"My dear Soulmate, I need a connection with you. A part of myself says, 'You're writing to him too much.' But the bigger part of me knows that to reach out to you is good. So, I open my mind and heart and invite you in. Welcome, Jim." I wrote this to Jim three weeks after our meeting. You can hear the echo of those dating games we're taught: "Don't pursue the man. Let him pursue you. Play it cool. Don't let them know how much you care." The problem with following such rules is that it's not honest. More important, it's not connected. And it's definitely not close. I took the risk to be open. I wanted closeness with Jim so badly, that I was laying myself bare, as much as I dared. Because he wanted as much closeness as I did, he didn't reject my connecting. No, he welcomed it and met me with his own yearning need. We're saying to you: Look for that in your soulmate. If, like us you're ready for your soulmate, you'll find that dating games are no fun.

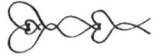 # August 17

Why Freedom Is Scary

Freedom. How scary it is. When you start getting free from your inner critic, you feel exhilarated. Then you feel fear. "I'm free. I can do anything." Yes. It was your inner critic that was keeping you in check—limiting your options. It told you that to live from your Natural Self was dangerous. We say: If you feel scared, you're doing it right! What we're saying is that the fear you feel when you start becoming liberated from your inner critic is merely the anxiety of entering a new psychological territory. We want to assure you that these feelings are perfectly natural. They will pass in a week or two. In their place will be a new philosophy of life—one guided by inner freedom, non-reactive love, and genuine caring.

 # August 18

Do You Need to Be Physically Attracted to Your Soulmate?

Do you need to be physically attracted to your soulmate? Short answer: Yes. That is, if your soulmate is your intimate sexual partner. It's not about movie-star good looks. It's that physical attraction is the end result of a stew of qualities in your partner that meld together into a powerful magnetic force. For me, it was Jim's intellect; his empathy; his strength; his maturity; his strong, graceful hands; his warm blue eyes that crinkled when he smiled; his broad shoulders; his nice butt; his incredible voice. Two arguments that often are posed against the necessity of physical attraction are that sex fades over time and that you should choose someone who you'd want as your best friend. To the first argument we say, not true. Research, along with our clinical experience say sex does not fade. It remains important into old age. We experienced that ourselves. As for the second argument, yes, the best-friend quality is essential but not sufficient. Without physical attraction, they'll remain your best friend, but not your soulmate lover. So, go ahead, add physical attraction to your criteria list. It's the magnet that will draw you to each other and keep you attached for your happily ever after.

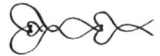 # August 19

How to Stop the Blame Game—Cold!

Blaming each other for not getting what you want. We know it seems as though others have done it to you. But we want to let you in on the secret behind blaming: It's a Power Giveaway! It puts your happiness in the hands of other people. If you're blaming others for not getting what you want or being who you want to be, the underlying reason is you have given away your power by believing a command from your Inner Critic. Let us translate a blaming statement for you as an example: "You won't let me have my feelings!" Translation: "I shouldn't feel what I'm feeling." How to stop the blame game cold? Get free from the Inner Critic command couched in that blaming statement. In this case, it's "I have the right to feel whatever I'm feeling." Just like that, you're free!

 # August 20

How to Stop Mood Swings

Ever feel like you're on an emotional roller coaster? One moment you're feeling great; the next someone says or does something and you've crashed into misery. The engine fueling these mood swings is your Inner Critic, making you dependent on buffers in order to feel good. A buffer is anything that props up your self-esteem. You feel as though you need these props because the Inner Critic is always at you, telling you you're defective, guilty, shameful, and inferior. To keep these negative feelings at bay, you compensate by amassing buffers. For example, you think, "I may not be pretty, but I have a good job." Or you feel one-down to your sibling so you console yourself with, "I have a boyfriend, and she doesn't." However, when you lose your job or your boyfriend, you're emotionally devastated, because you've lost your buffer against your Inner Critic's condemnation of you. As you continually gain and lose external props to your self-esteem, your moods swing wildly. How do you get off this roller coaster? Get free from your Inner Critic by no longer believing its messages. You can begin today with this challenge: "My worth is a given. Nothing I do could take that away."

 # August 21

You've Touched My Very Soul

"You've touched my very soul." It's a line from a song I heard. It got me thinking. A high-voltage soulmate love is more than physical attraction; more than intellectual compatibility. It's a spiritual bond. When you're falling into a pattern of ho-humness about your relationship, or more painful, when you're in a pattern of fighting with each other, think of this: We have to make a values choice. Do we want to see each other as adversaries or as spiritual beings on a soulmate journey with each other?

 # August 22

How to Find Your Voice

"Okay, silence. Yes, I was silenced. Be a good little boy, and shut up. And then those bastards would ask, 'What's the matter? Cat got your tongue?'" Jim shared this experience in a letter to me. Many people we see in our therapy practice had this experience too. The net result of this kind of treatment is that you develop a block to speaking your voice in relationships. We want to encourage you about this. Here's what Jim did: "I said to myself, 'If they can do it, I can learn it. Even though I didn't know how.'" And he did. You can learn it too. It will mean taking a risk with others to let yourself put into words what your mind is thinking. Like Jim, you will find your voice. And with your partner, you will create closeness.

 # August 23

Don't Get Skunked in Relationships

Our little dog Libby was a hunter. She got skunked four times one year. She just couldn't help herself. She felt compelled to chase a skunk. However, when it was all over, she came home with tears in her eyes and smelling horrible. Maybe you've felt compelled to pursue a certain kind of partner who isn't good for you. You know those partners who leave you in tears and with the stench of a painful relationship to add to your history. In Anthetic Therapy, we call such a compulsion a *replay*. This is a pattern of choosing in adulthood a partner who repeats the pain of an earlier, usually childhood relationship. Fortunately, we have an advantage over Libby. We can analyze our destructive patterns and learn from them. We have executive self-functioning from which to draw strength to break free from our replays. Once we get free from our patterns, we no longer chase skunky relationships. In fact, we clear the path for our soulmate. We wish such freedom for you today.

 # August 24

Failure of the Men in Our Lives:
A New Perspective

"Failure of male authorities. Daddy. Boyfriends. Pastors. Yes, sweet Kathy—all painful failures of external supports, and so necessary so that you could find your own voice." When Jim wrote this to me in an early letter, I was trying to come to terms with my history: longing for men in my life to be reliable, connecting, supporting—and all of them coming up short. Jim helped me have a new perspective. Yes, men had failed me, but because they had, I had found my own strength; my own voice. Perhaps men in your life have failed you too. Painful as that is, look for the gifts: You developed your own selfhood and strength.

 # August 25

Reduce Your Concern about What Other People Think

Thinking of doing something different? New hairstyle? Going back to school? New relationship? Then have you felt keenly aware, "What will other people think?" That thought comes from your Inner Critic—doing its best to make you conform so as not to trigger other people's criticism. When you pretzelize yourself to please other people, you give away your power to do what you want. Here are two challenges to your Inner Critic to help you reduce your concern about what other people think: "I have the right to do *what I want; not pretzelize myself to please other people*" and "*I no longer choose to give my power away to other people.*" Now you're set to have a soul-fulfilling day.

 # August 26

Cathexis: The Core of Soulmate Love

Cathexis: It's a term that means holding someone in your heart. It's a core sign of soulmate love. You see some item in a store and think, "Oh, he would love this!" You eat a delicious restaurant meal and think, "I have to tell him about this; he will like it too." You travel to a beautiful place and muse, "Oh, I wish he were here with me." They are always with you; always on your mind and in your heart. Let this be added to your criteria list: Do they come to my mind unbidden? Do I want to share everything with them? And watch for what they tell you: Are they quick to tell you how you were in their heart while they were away?

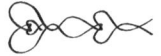 # August 27

Want Trust in Your Relationship?

Want a relationship in which you trust each other? Or want to restore trust that's been lost? There's one secret ingredient that will do it: *honesty*. We mean tell your partner about your feelings; likes and dislikes. Also, tell them what you've been thinking and doing. We know this is counter to conventional wisdom that says, "Don't upset your partner by telling the truth." From our years of counseling couples, we know that this strategy will get you one thing: distance. Not trust. And definitely not closeness. We also know what holds people back from honesty. It's thinking, "If I were honest, it would hurt my partner's feelings. It might make my partner angry. My partner might throw it in my face later. We'd just have a fight." It all comes down to this. You have to decide on a basic value: Do I want a High-Voltage Relationship or a Low-Voltage Relationship? Do I want closeness or distance? Choosing honesty and high-voltage relationship might come with repercussions. It's a risk. But the alternative is distrust and distance. Besides, the repercussions can be processed. So, our advice to you today: Choose honesty, and let the chips fall where they may.

 # August 28

Men: What to Do if She's Depressed

"He hates it when I'm depressed. He doesn't know what to do." Said by one of my recent female counseling clients. But I've heard it from many. So, men, here's some help for you in handling your woman when she's down. First, what not to do: Don't withdraw. Don't say, "Snap out of it." Instead, ask her, "Can you tell me what you're feeling?" Then, just listen. Next, ask her, "Is there anything you'd like from me?" Finally, take her in your arms, and tell her, "I'm here for you. I love you. Everything is going to be alright." There. Now, you're equipped.

 # August 29

Feel Irritable? Here's Why

Been feeling irritable lately? Like any little thing could set you off? You know how it goes. First, you feel a little unsettled. Then, a little aggravated. Next thing you know, you're biting your loved one's head off over the smallest thing. You're puzzled. So, you think, "Must be the stress I'm under at work." We want to let you in on the secret to why we can feel irritable. It's that you've submerged your Natural Self energies. Whole parts of yourself condemned to be locked away in your subconscious. Why? Because if they were to emerge into consciousness, your Inner Critic would pounce. You'd feel scared, depressed. But these powerful energies can't be submerged for long. They emerge in disguised form. Hence, your irritability. Here's how to get free: Label it, "This is a clue I've been constricting myself at the hands of my Inner Critic." Then ask yourself, "What is it I've been feeling or desiring that I won't let myself look at?" Let those inklings of the answer emerge fully into your awareness. As you attend to them, your irritability will vanish. You can enjoy your life—and your relationships—in peace.

 # August 30

Can You Accept Compliments?

Ever responded to a compliment on something you're wearing with, "Oh, this old thing? I got it on sale!"? Ever quipped in response to someone praising you about an achievement, "I was just lucky"? This is what we call *praise deflection*. Guess who's behind it? If you said, "My Inner Critic," you were right! Its goal: To safeguard you against the danger of thinking too well of yourself. Net result: You miss out on the pleasure of agreeing with someone who gives you a compliment. The antidote? Say to your Inner Critic, "I have the right to accept compliments; even to agree with them." Believe it. We want you to have this pleasure.

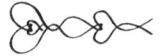 # August 31

Have Trouble Taking Orders?

Do you have trouble taking orders? Following someone's instructions? Can't stop and ask for directions when you're lost? Want to understand yourself? Difficulty submitting to others or being influenced by others (and that's what this is about), is because your power and autonomy buffers might collapse. A buffer is anything that props up our self-esteem. We get attached to buffers to keep the pain of our Inner Critic's punishments at bay. You know, those feelings of defectiveness, shame, guilt, and inferiority. As long as we feel powerful or independent, we have a shield up against the pain. But there's a better way to get free from Inner Critic pain. That's to take back your rights. In this case, it's "I have the right to submit to someone; to take orders, to do exactly what they're asking. Submission doesn't change my worth as a person in the least."

September 1

Are There Only a Few Good Men?

She stayed in a painful relationship. It was one she admitted was no good for her. She reasoned, "There are so few good men out there. If I give up this relationship, I'll never find another one as good." Why do we stay in a relationship with the wrong person? Dr. James Elliott explains in *Disarming Your Inner Critic*, "You think you might be able to convert this flawed person into someone who is not only successful and effective but who really does love you. On top of this, your Inner Critic tells you that if you give up pursuing him or her, you'll never find another one as good. Your Inner Critic is just interested in protecting you from the riskiness of giving and receiving genuine love." This boils down to that we stay in a dead-end relationship at the hands of our Inner Critic. The good news is that we can get free. Our stuckness stems from just one more magnified fear generated by our Inner Critic. Don't give that fear the power of belief. The Inner Critic has no idea what it's talking about. There are plenty good men out there. And there's one just for you.

September 2

You Are My Michelangelo

Did you know you are a sculptor for your partner? Relationship researcher Caryl Rusbult found, if all goes well, partners sculpt each other to help them become the person each aspires to be; in fact, the ideal that each desires for himself or herself. After only five days of knowing him, I asked Jim to inseminate me! I said, "I have a request that you inseminate me with your strength, with a belief in myself." He continued that process over the entire course of our marriage, teaching me the skills for becoming strong; for becoming the person I ideally wanted to be. So, I say, "Jim, you are my Michelangelo. You have sculpted me and brought out the best in me that I aspired to." I share this with you so that you may assess any potential partner: "Do they affirm me and help me become, not what others think I should be, but what I would love to be?" If you're already in a relationship, you can help your partner in this unique way: Hear their heart's desire for what they long to become. Then affirm and support them in doing just that. Rusbult says here's the true test: If your partner is being your Michelangelo, you will feel exhilarated." I can attest to that!

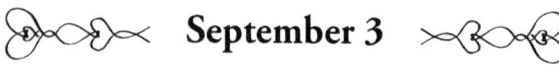

September 3

What to Do after the First Date

Wow! Your first date went well! Now what? I want to share with you what Jim and I did. We considered our ten-day doctoral meeting our "first date." What we did was talk about it—to each other. At length. Listen to Jim's letter written about the night we parted: "As I lay in bed, all kinds of images came to me—your dear face, your empowering words, the song you sang." (He was bringing up the images of our meeting that stayed with him.) You can do that too. Then he told me the impact on him our meeting had produced: "I was driving to go shopping for groceries, and a car cut in front of me. I was about to get angry when I said, 'Wait a minute.' And I was now speaking from some deep place in me, and the episode of the other driver now seemed quite insignificant; just a little ripple way up there, not very important at all, and I could love the driver of the other car. So, I now felt that serenity that I hadn't known at all that I was lacking. And you had evoked that in me." Here, Jim put into words how I had affected him, even changed him. You can do that too. So, if you're wondering what to do after the first date, we say, talk about it. Review with each other the scenes left in your mind. Most important, put into words how that experience has impacted you. Do these things, and you'll be creating your high-voltage soulmate relationship.

September 4

When We're Beheld, We Grow

When we're alone, we often don't see ourselves. We need each other to see who we really are. Let me give you an example from our lives. When Jim and I were parting at the airport, he had parked the car away from the terminal near the trees. With another hour or two before my flight, we had sat in the car and talked and talked. At one point. The security guards tapped on Jim's window and asked if everything was okay. I felt guilty (for no reason, of course). But, Jim handled it with such strength and maturity, I just loved him for it. I told him so in one of my first letters to him. Doing so had a big impact on Jim. He wrote: "I love feedback from you; for example, about the security guard at the airport. To me that seemed quite ordinary, what I did. Your writing about it gave me a new perspective on myself." So, that was it. In being beheld, we each began to see ourselves in a new light. "So that's me? That strong man that she sees?" Yes, that's you. When you see yourself through my eyes, you glimpse your magnificence.

September 5

Proud? That Can Cause Arguments

"Are you going to put that much salt in the stew?" Jim asked me. I puffed up defensively. "I've been cooking this dish for years! I've always put this much salt." I was proud of being a good cook. So, I was ready for an argument when Jim asked his question. I know I'm not alone in this. There's also, "I'm proud of my ability to make money," "I'm proud of how I keep house," even "I'm proud of being a caring person." While pride may seem like a worthy goal, it can also have some drawbacks. Because pride is a buffer. We rely on it to keep our Inner Critic at bay. And there's the problem. We'll defend the object of our pride to the death. Without our pride, we'd feel defective, inferior. That's why we'll argue about it with our partner. Want to nip that argument in the bud? 1) Recognize that your defensiveness is a clue that this item is not just something you like about yourself. It's a buffer. 2) See that there's an Inner Critic should attached to it. For example, "I should be a perfect cook." 3) Get free by saying to your Inner Critic, "I have the right to be an imperfect cook, even a bad cook!" Do these things, and peace will reign in your house. Not only that, you might learn a thing or two from your partner.

September 6

Time on Your Hands? How to Enjoy It

"Well, I carved out this time for myself—no responsibilities—*now* what do I do?" Here's the key: Tap your Natural Self. That means getting in touch with what sparks you. You can sit quietly to access it or you can wander around aimlessly. The point is pay attention to your inner world. Does a little thought enter your mind, "Ooh, that might be interesting"? That's a spark. Does a stronger impulse nudge at you, "Oh, my gosh, that would be so wonderful to do"? That's a spark too. If you're a couple, tell each other, "You know what? I'd like to… Would you join me?" We have one more suggestion: Connect. With your feelings. Share those feelings about yourself, about life, about each other—with each other. In short, follow those sparks! You'll cure boredom. You're sure to enjoy the day.

September 7

Your Relationship: Safe Haven or Combat Zone?

There's no getting around it. Conflict is going to happen in your relationship. So, how do you cope? Low-Voltage partners usually rely on one of three options: fighting, submitting, or distancing. They have to avoid closeness, because they lack skills. If they get too close, they often end up in a bitter argument. That's a combat relationship—one where verbal attacks have become accepted as normal. High-Voltage couples, on the other hand, have learned skills for successfully resolving conflict. That created a safe haven. Safe enough to talk about anything—especially feelings. How can you tell if you're creating a safe haven? You'll enjoy emotional closeness, soft-heartedness, and love. It all comes down to a basic values choice: Do you choose a safe haven or a combat zone?

September 8

You'll Need One Word to Get Closeness—and a Happy Partner

Want more closeness? There's one word that will go a long way to producing it. That word is "Yes!" Saying "Yes" to easy-to-do requests is an important ingredient in closeness. Why? Because you'll not only be making your partner happy by fulfilling their desires, you'll be living from a caring part of yourself. That's a part who can empathize with your partner's pleasure. Now, to say Yes, you're going to need to be free. That is, free from psychological blocks such a self-centeredness and hard-heartedness. In short, you'll need to get free from your Inner Critic's condemnation of your surrendering to love. So, today, listen to your partner's requests. Then, try saying, "Yes!" Closeness will be your reward.

September 9

Red Flags to Relationship Trouble

Red flags. They're behaviors that are early warning signs to relationship trouble on the horizon. He might be a chronic flirt with other women while you're dating. It's a predictor of infidelity once you're married. She might say, "Don't let me cut and run." It's a clue she'll be withdrawing and distancing. He might push you, take your car keys, restrain you. It's a good chance he'll escalate into worse abuse. We know it's a temptation in the blush of early love to want to overlook each red flag. Your black hole that longs for love will want to turn a blind eye to the pain these red flags are already causing you. We recommend you take executive charge of your black hole. Be alert. At the least, the red flag is an indicator you need to request your partner get therapy for these behaviors. At the most, you need to scratch this person off your list. Make way for a partner who treats you lovingly and with respect. If you find this hard to do, we recommend you get counseling to help you break free from your drivenness to put up with pain. We want you to be free!

September 10

No Name Calling!

"Numnutz!" "Old Fart!" If you've gotten into a pattern of calling your partner such names, that's a clue that you've got some unprocessed anger toward your partner. What's more, it's turned into an attitude of disrespect. That's not funny. It's corrosive. We're not going to tell you to just stop it. That's not enough. You need to analyze the anger that's driving it. For example, "Have I been silencing my voice about my needs?" "Have I failed to translate my anger into neutral requests of my partner?" There are others, of course, but this will get you started. We want you to be free of anger, to be at peace, and to be happy. Most important, we want you to have closeness. So, today, start with No Name Calling!

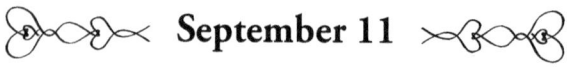

September 11

So Little Time Together? What to Do

"We have so little time together. It's hard to connect." If you're dealing with that challenge, here's what we say: You can take those few minutes you *do* have and turn them into a deep connection that sustains you all day. It takes two steps: One, avoid using that time to talk about items external to your relationship, such as the news, the neighbors, the chores. Two, use that time to talk about what you mean to each other. When Jim and I were 2,000 miles apart, before internet and cell phones, we would dive into our phone calls by talking about what we meant to each other. Jim told me, "When I look in my post office box and there is a letter from you, I begin to feel a glow that starts in my chest and spreads throughout my body. As I read your letter, I have a vivid sense of your sweet presence." You can use Jim's words as a guide. Say to your partner, "When I look at you (getting the kids ready, waking up beside me, feeding the dog), I begin to feel (warm, loving, proud, in awe), and I fall in love with you all over again." Your partner will feel as I felt; warmed, loved, cherished. Those few minutes shared with Jim, and I walked on a cloud. You will too.

September 12

What Do Women Want—and Need?

"Yes, I am both gentle and strong. My male strength is here for you whenever you want it. I will be careful to ensure your tiniest qualm will get my full care and attention. It will be a deep pleasure for me." (Jim's words to me early on.) Can you see how I was transported with love and valuing of this man? He was giving me the two things modern women want: masculine strength paired with gentleness and sensitivity. How does a man develop these qualities? By doing what Jim did: developing his tolerance for strong emotions in himself and others. Learning to note them as they bubbled up and just observing them. "Oh, there's some pain. There's some sadness. There's some anger. I can just let them be what they are; I don't have to do anything about them." Then learn to take pleasure in caring. Feel the good feelings that come with connecting with another with love. Cultivate these, and you will be a man that women have to have.

September 13

Women, Are You Afraid of Men?

"What about women's resistance to men? I think it is a fear of losing themselves. Oppressed by male logic, they distrust it." Those were Jim's words to me in an early letter. And, he offered a solution: "As long as women feel unassertive and helpless, they will distrust and resist male reasoning and logic. What they need to do, it seems to me, is learn to reason; to think critically. Then they will no longer be oppressed by male authorities. They will have weapons to resist. And need not fear maleness." So, I took Jim up on this. I learned critical thinking skills. And the fear had no power over me. Try it, my dear sister.

September 14

The Secret to Feeling Secure in Your Relationship

Want to know the secret to creating security in relationships? I named it in an early card to Jim: "This morning I'm meditating on your *devoted availability* to me." How did Jim do it? "You arrange your schedule to receive my calls (and you never ever act sacrificial about it), and you leave your phone on all night when you know I might need you. I know absolutely that I can call you anytime, and your voice, when it hears mine on the other end, will turn all warm and delighted and say, 'Aw, Kathy.'" So, if you want to create security, or if you're trying to assess whether a person will provide you with that security, observe whether they are *there* for you. As I told Jim, "To be *assured* of a loving welcome is a wonderful thing."

September 15

Clue to Recognizing Your Soulmate

"I'd rather fight with you than make love with anyone else." This was the climactic line in "The Wedding Date," a movie Jim and I loved to watch. As we held hands, Jim in his hospital bed and I beside him I said to him, "I'd rather sit here and watch movies with you than be out galivanting with anyone else." He nodded. That's an important clue to recognizing your soulmate. Would you rather be doing *anything* at all with your partner than doing something grand with anyone else? If you can answer "Yes!" you have an essential confirmation.

September 16

How to Handle Criticism of Your Relationship

"You need to find a man who has a 9 to 5 job," they told her. "You'll be eating crumbs off the first wife's table," they predicted. Sound familiar? Have you had to face others' criticism of your choice of partner or of your relationship? Did it make you doubt yourself or your partner? We know about this. Jim and I had to face criticism over and over before we got married. Fortunately, my wise Jim knew how to handle it. "You have to use critical thinking skills," he said. That means you question and evaluate what your critics are saying. You also need to have clear criteria for the life partner you want. Then you'll have an internal compass to direct your choice. And so, give you confidence. You'll have the strength to stand together. Against the world if necessary. Here's to your clarity and strength!

September 17

Your Soulmate: Twins Yet Different

How can you recognize your soulmate? Jim captured it in his early letter to me: "I am aware more and more that what attracts me to you is the fact that you are my counterpart and that no one else even comes close to being that. At the same time, you are someone other than me. First, you are female, with all the magic and mystery and fascination that that entails for me. Second, you have a more highly developed spirituality than I, so I am getting constant surprises from you. Third, that you are Southern. And fourth, a whole bunch of other things. So, you are my identical twin but not a carbon copy. Sufficiently identical for us to fall into each other; sufficiently different for us to be constantly surprised by each other." There you have it. You'll know your soulmate by two things: how much alike you are and how you are surprised by each other. As Jim said, "It's a nice combination."

September 18

How to Wait for Your Soulmate

She's waiting for her soulmate. She's not settling. So, she bought a box. It's an intriguing, decorative box, sort of antique-looking travel box with an old-fashioned handle. One side has an ancient globe on it with the words, "Life is a journey; love is what makes the journey worthwhile." She's using her box as a container for thoughts, clippings, and items that represent her soulmate quest and that she wants to share with him when he arrives. Jim did a version of this as he waited for his soulmate. He made a scrapbook. In it he put poems, cartoons, clippings about love. The poems he read to me at our first lovemaking. They became part of our wedding ceremony. If you're waiting for your soulmate, you can do this too. Save the special quotes, poems, items that represent your search and your hope. They'll bless you and become a source of celebration when you and your soulmate find each other. They'll enrich your fulfillment.

September 19

Your Love Keeps Me Warm

I went through a surgery not long ago. It's not an easy thing to face. In fact, it's one of those times when life presents us with a chill. But at every step, I was enfolded in love and kindness. In pre-op, they had warm blankets waiting on the foot of my bed. More important, I was wrapped in the love of friends, family, and underneath it all, Jim. I like the way he wrote about this early on in our relationship: "I am wrapped in your love. Surrounded and supported by your total acceptance of me. Your love keeps me warm. It embraces me, holds me close, warms my soul. So even though you are miles away, I am comforted. Your steadfast affection and loyalty hover over me, protect me." If you're in an intimate relationship, enfold each other. If you're soulmate questing, search for the one whose accepting, steadfast love keeps you warm.

September 20

Like It? Say It!

You know you've done it a million times. You liked something your partner did—but never said a word. Here's your tip for today: If your partner is doing something you like, it's absolutely essential for closeness that you say it to them. Here's what Jim told me during our first months: "I like it when I give you some feedback (e.g., 'I like such-and-such that you said') and you say, 'That's important for me to hear. Please do as much of this as you possibly can.'" So, I did. And it's a tried and true formula. Like it? Say it! You're gonna get bliss!

September 21

What Anger Is Really About

You've seen baboons charge, right? Arms rigid. Chest out. Nostrils huffing. We humans do that too—or some version of it when we're angry. It's scary. And it's meant to be. Translated it says, "I'm feeling threatened. Afraid I'm being attacked. I'm going to protect myself by scaring you with my anger." Want to know what their anger is *really* about? It's that they're trying to ward off an Inner Critic event. I learned this personally by experiencing it myself. When our Inner Critic pounces, it makes us feel terrible emotionally; so terrible that we'll do anything to stop it. That includes resorting to anger to scare our partner who is triggering our Inner Critic, often by such innocent behavior as making a request of us. We have a solution the baboon does not: We can use our evolved brain to challenge our Inner Critic. Then we don't have to resort to anger. Ah! Peace will reign.

September 22

The Power of Speaking Their Name

"Stay near me. Speak my name." Those lines are from the poem, "Midcentury Love Letter;" very special to us. That second sentence is what we want to point out to you today. Specifically, that there is power in speaking your partner's name. Business people know this principle. We all love to hear our name. Now here's a variation on that for lovers. Get in touch with your adoration of your beloved, and then whisper—yes, whisper their name in their ear—four times. It's magical. Here's how I wrote in my letter to Jim a month before our marriage: "Oh, Jim, I hold you in my arms and hear you lose yourself in a litany of whispered 'Kathys.'" It was profound. If you try this, you'll experience the deepest power of speaking their name.

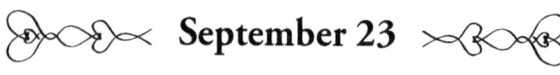

September 23

**Your Cover Story:
It Could Prevent Your Growth**

"That's just the way I am;" "If I were to change, I wouldn't be me." "I don't need therapy; I'm doing okay the way I am, well, except for the fact my relationships don't work." Sound familiar? These are all examples of the cover story we create to explain the problems our Inner Critic produces. In Anthetic Therapy, we label our cover story a *buffer*. It keeps at bay the emotional pain our Inner Critic induces. We're here to tell you, you don't need a cover story. Your worth as a person is a given. You never have to create a fiction to prove you're a good person. You can present yourself to the world just as you are—no cover.

September 24

Decoding "I Don't Like to Talk about Feelings"

"I don't like to talk about feelings." This statement is not what it appears—a simple statement of dislike. You'll need to decode this one. It actually is a symptom of thymophobia, which means a fear of feelings. We all have a certain amount of this problem. For example, you may find it easy to cry but have trouble expressing anger. Or you may find it easy to express anger but difficult to express hurt. In each case, the avoidance of feelings is driven by trying to avoid the Inner Critic induced pain you'd feel if you dared to express that feeling. Not only does thymophobia block our personal growth, it also blocks closeness. Because when we can't confront a feeling, we don't want to listen when others talk about *their* feelings. So, to get free, take back your right to feel *everything*! Come alive!

September 25

Play with the Child in Each Other

"I want to take you somewhere to show you something I think you'll really like." That was Jim to me the week we met. He drove a few blocks and parked the car at a building as yet a mystery to me. As we walked from the car to that building, I could begin to see what was inside. It was a carousel! Oh, my! This man truly was seeing that inner child that longed for a man to see her; to play with her; to love her. It was magical. Here are the high-voltage soulmate elements of what Jim did: 1) He beheld me in depth. Took in that I was in touch with a child part who loved things like stuffed animals. 2) He took time to think of something that would thrill that inner child in me. 3) He initiated taking me there. 4) He played with me. You can learn from Jim. Follow his lead. Behold the child in your partner. Think of what you could do that would please that child. Then play together. It will be a heart-touching experience.

September 26

The Deeper Meaning of Sex

After only six days of knowing Jim, I made an outrageous request of him. I asked him to inseminate me! I explained that I was asking for him to imbue me with his presence, his strength; with a belief in myself. From my first sight of him, I had seen his personal power, and I wanted that essence of who he was inside me. Not surprisingly, after I dared to speak it, my Inner Critic pounced. I told Jim, "I'm afraid you'll see my request as a physical come-on. My Inner Critic says it's phony; it's just sex I'm wanting." In response, Jim taught me an important perspective: "But even if physical sex were to be involved, it would be symbolic of deeper insemination." You know, Jim was right. At its best, sex is not just a physical act. It is an expression of the merging of heart, soul, and body of the two lovers.

September 27

Endings: How to Make Them Wonderful

Endings can be hard. Even painful. Whether it's the last day of vacation or of college; of a career or of a life together, when you've loved the experience, it can be heart-wrenching for it to end. But the way Jim and I spent the last day of our meeting experience may be helpful for you when you face those inevitable ends of things. That meeting had it all, everything we each loved—intellectual sharing, the beauty of the ocean, cozy fires, great food. But most important, it had our meeting; our Finding each other at last. That final night was a celebration of all this. Jim and I and our fellow learners and faculty gathered in our meeting room in chairs or on the floor; a warm fire crackling in the fireplace. We talked about our impressions of each other and of what the experience had meant to each of us. Then we began to sing! Song after song; songs of joy; songs of blessing. I was on a cloud. Here are the elements you can use: Talk directly to each other of your impressions. Savor what the experience has meant to you; speak of it to each other. Sing to each other. Bless each other. You will make that ending wonderful.

September 28

Tip for How to Recognize Your Soulmate

Here's a tip for how to recognize your soulmate. There's a realization; in fact, a revelation that will emerge in your mind. You'll marvel, "I have never loved like this before." I know Jim and I each wrote those words to each other during the first six months of our relationship. Oh, you may have loved before even deeply. But the love you feel for your soulmate is deeper yet. It's at the soul level, deeper than you've ever been. It will have an element of surprise and even awe for you. It must be mutual, of course, for the relationship to develop. And, you'll need skills. With such soulmate love and the skills for creating closeness, you'll be well on your way to ecstasy.

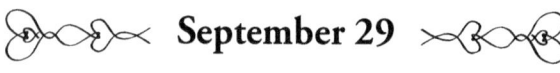

September 29

Want Closeness?
You Have to Be a Researcher

Odd as it may sound, to have closeness in your relationship, you have to be a researcher. Now, don't panic. You won't need to know statistics, you'll just need a few simple skills. You'll need to employ these skills whenever your partner gives you feedback. For example, Jim told me, "You seem touchy." Now, my impulse was to automatically deny it with, "No, I'm not touchy!" But, Jim taught me to say, "Can you tell me more about that?" And even to say, "Can you say what I'm doing that leads you to say that?" Once you learn to respond to feedback in this way, you'll reap three dividends: One, you'll have a chance to learn about yourself. Two, you'll have the opportunity for elements in your personality to emerge and be accepted by you. And three, using Anthetic inner critic releasing statements, you'll get free from some self-condemnation and constrictedness. Oh, and as an added dividend you'll get closeness with your partner. So, be a Researcher!

September 30

Feeling Off-Center? Anxious? What to Do

"I applaud the way you're dealing with your feelings of being off-center and your anxiety and feelings of unrest. I want to assure you again that these are signs of impending growth, and you are accepting and integrating them instead of making them go away." These were Jim's words to me in the early part of our relationship; a time of great upheaval and change in my life. Are you, too, going through such a time? If so, I offer you the reassurance Jim gave me. It's the perspective that everything we feel is acceptable. It may seem counter-intuitive, but the strategy Jim taught me has proved true: "Keep encouraging your jangly feelings to bubble up; they will inevitably lead to growth."

October 1

Soulmates Are Permeable

Permeable. It means literally "having pores or openings that liquids or gases can pass through" (Webster's Dictionary). It's a good word to describe the quality needed to have a high-voltage soulmate relationship. Being open to each other. Letting in concepts, feelings, and of course, love. I wrote Jim in my love letter two weeks after we met, "Your permeability idea is beautiful. Yes, we are permeable to each other. Yes, it is a joy." To be permeable, you'll need to assess that your partner relates to you in an accepting, non-judgmental, loving, caring way. Once you see that they are those things, you can open yourself. It will be bliss.

 # October 2

Emotional Connection; Deeper Sex

"I have this sense that seeing you again, looking each other in the eye, and your holding my face in your hands would be enough to bring me to orgasm (no genital touching necessary)." I wrote that to Jim one month after our meeting. I'm sharing it today, because I hope it will encourage you about deepening your sexual connection. It's not about being a good technician; it's about being a good connector. I continued "That's how deeply you touch me. And that's a tribute to you and the quality with which you relate to me that I could be moved so deeply by the emotional/spiritual interchange with you." So, if you'd like this too, start by telling each other what a treasure they are to you. Be specific. Let your heart gush words of valuing of the other. It will lead to a profound connection in your heart, your soul, and your body.

October 3

Decision to Make? How to Make It Good

Do you have a decision to make? Maybe about a life partner, a job, or some other action to take. Here's a tip to help you make a good decision: Be systematic. Not impulsive. Do research—pros and cons. Analyze consequences. Don't decide when you're feeling angry or fearful. Make a list of your ideal for this situation. Check how well this decision matches your ideal. The closer the match, the more likely you'll be satisfied with the outcome. Oh, and one more thing. Once you've systematically made your decision, be at peace. You can always edit. By that we mean, most decisions can be corrected. For any that can't, you can merely get free from any Inner Critic put-downs about yourself. Everything's going to be okay.

 # October 4

Does Marriage Make Us Happy?

That is a question lurking around the issue of marriage. The answer: "It's not marriage that makes you happy. It's happy marriage that makes you happy." So spoke Harvard researcher Dr. Daniel Gilbert. He added, "The single best predictor of human happiness is the quality of social relationships." Our work in Anthetic Relationship Therapy has produced a model to guide you in producing a happy relationship: The High-Voltage Relationship model. Its goal: *optimality*. Optimal relating involves a two-pronged approach: skills for psychological growth of each partner and skills for deep expressive love. We want you to be happy.

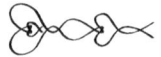 # October 5

Is it OK to be Obsessed with Your Partner?

"I think about you constantly (I mean every single minute, except when I'm with a client)." Jim's words two months after we met. Obsession? Yes. He added, "I understand quite well your fear of saying you want so much of me that you will scare me away." I was obsessed too. Was that okay? You bet. Here's how Jim described it: "Right now we are in a very intense phase of our relationship, an obsessive phase, and rightly so. We are two very intensely feeling, very sensitive, very responsive people. What we are doing now is building our relationship, letting our neediness show (risking it: Can I really let the other see how strongly I feel?); actually checking each other out to see if the other can stand the power of our emotions. We are not wishy-washy people. We love fiercely, extravagantly. But each of us is quite strong. Each of us can confront great intensities of feeling. As we test the acceptance of the other, we will begin to feel more and more secure." And we did. That obsessiveness became a steady glow of security, love, and acceptance that sustained us for 22 years. So, take us as your guide. Obsessing is fine; even desirable. Just check to make sure that it's mutual. It's a furnace that will have you both glowing.

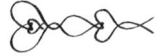 # October 6

The Power of Positive Speaking

It's no surprise that researchers have found that speaking positively to each other is a key ingredient in happy marriages. However, researchers also found that it's hard for couples to do it. Why is this? In our therapy, we found that positivity has to contain 2 essential ingredients. One, it has to be specific to your partner. Two, it must be focused on elements about which your partner values being seen. Here are a few specific prompts for you to use in expressing positivity: "I like it when you…" "I really admire your…" "Thanks for being so…" Each of these when the sentence is completed is a positive stroke for your partner. They are part of the glue that holds your high-voltage relationship together.

 # October 7

5 Judgmental Phrases to Delete from Your Vocabulary

They're little things. Hardly anything to take notice of. Those little judgmental phrases we sprinkle in our conversations. Problem is they hurt. And when we use them with our loved ones they destroy closeness. Here are 5 of them to delete from your vocabulary: "I can't believe you did that;" "You didn't even;" "You ought to be *ashamed* of yourself;" "The *least* you could do;" "How is your *little* project going?" How can you delete these corrosive phrases? One, monitor yourself for pulls to say them. Two, do impulse control. You can overcome blurting them out. Your relationships will benefit. We promise.

 # October 8

Beware the Inner Critic Police

"As you get free from your Inner Critic and begin to live from your natural self, other people may not approve. You may find that others try to police you back into your old reactive life style. They may call you self-centered and selfish simply because you are no longer putting them first." Underlying their anger at you may be the message, "How dare you get away with being free when I'm not able to." Our message to you is, don't let the Inner Critic Police get you down. You have the right to decide how you will live your life.

 # October 9

5 Ways to Sweeten Your Relationship

"My sweet girl. And you *are* sweet. How nice to have someone who is not contentious, judgmental, jangly! And who is accepting. And who is committed to resolving conflicts not by escalating them and acting out but by working on stuff, as I am. You are so perfect for me, it takes my breath away when I think of all the ways you are." Ooh, Jim's letter to me thrilled me. And he offered us an outline of 5 ways we can all sweeten our relationships: 1) Don't be contentious; 2) don't be judgmental; 3) don't be jangly; 4) be accepting; and 5) resolve conflicts not by escalating them and acting out your upset, but by working on the stuff that's driving them. Do these 5 things, and it will leave you—breathless.

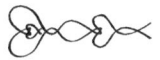 # October 10

What's Wrong with Saying "Too Late!"

You know how you can long to get something from a partner—maybe diamond earrings; maybe a weekend vacation together; maybe a simple, "I love you"? And months or years go by without the slightest sign that you'll receive it? Then one day, there it is! Your partner comes through: The gift-wrapped box with those sparkling earrings; the tickets and reservations to that cherished spot; the sound of those tender words in your ear. And what are you tempted to say? "Too late! You should have done this years ago." It would be such sweet revenge. But unless you want to end the relationship, don't say it! Why? Because it's revenge. And revenge is a closeness-killer. Plus, it's cold comfort. Instead, let the goodness of this moment sink in. Say, "Thank you. That means so much to me." Then, let the sweet pleasure draw you closer.

October 11

Arguments: Should You Break Up?

They're like Eden—those first months of your relationship. Then an argument (what Jim and I call a "glitch") occurs. Such trouble in paradise can really rock your relationship. Four months into our relationship Jim wrote, "The closer one gets (the more merged) the more skills people need, because stuff will get triggered if we get close." So, be encouraged, dear one, if you're aiming for closeness, you will have arguments. We all have land mines of emotional pain that will blow up when our partner is close enough to trip the mechanism. Here's what you need: skills. Skills for working with anger and hurt. As Jim said, "We are equal to the task: we know how to deal with the tangles. That is more precious to me than gold and rubies." So, are you wondering if those arguments you're having mean that you should break up? Before you answer that, learn these skills, apply them during your glitches. See if you don't create a new Eden.

 # October 12

Surprises May Have a Spiritual Source

"I am so grateful we had the extra hour together." Here I am writing to Jim in 1989 about a wonderful thing that occurred when we were parting in the Dallas airport after having spent five days together. We would board separate planes to fly back to our homes 2,000 miles distant from each other. We did not want to part. We had just consummated our sexual relationship. And during that time decided we wanted to get married. We were saying our goodbyes when the airline announced that my flight was delayed: We would have another hour together. Here's how I interpreted that serendipitous hour: "Surely we have an indulgent God, who smiles on us, surrounds our lovemaking, then says, 'My children, have an extra hour together. I give it to you freely.'" Twenty-two years later, as I re-read that letter, it gave me a new perspective on the last years of our life. Jim's stroke in 2008 was not the end of his life. We had three more years together before his death. Again, I sense the work of an indulgent god. I want to pass this idea on to you. How is that indulgent god working in your life and relationship?

 # October 13

Don't Wait for the Right Time

"I'm waiting for the right time to talk to him about it." We can't tell you how many times we've heard those words. Our advice? Don't wait for the "right" time. Jim's early letter to me explains why: "How pleased I am at the way we bring up issues and glitches and process them immediately (I know there's nothing seething inside, and that makes me feel calm and secure)." So that's it. When you talk about feelings as they come up, you're no longer sitting with it inside, where you'll start to seethe about it. Like us, you will feel calm and secure.

 # October 14

How Do You Know Whether to Take the Risk?

They met in a crowd. Recognized each other from long ago. She told me she reflected on whether to dive into this relationship. An inner guiding part said, "Life is urgent." She told me, "The vibes were good enough that I could take that risk." And they did. She mused, "If I could create a fantasy relationship, this would be it. It is excellent." What do I see in her? She followed her spark to go to the event, met him, felt the attraction. Then she used her rational mind to assess, "Is this a good risk?" He passed the test.

October 15

Connect the Dots: Self-Acceptance…Closeness

You have Inner Critic shoulds that keep whole parts of your personality submerged. Locked away. If they try to emerge, the feelings of defectiveness lead you to push them back down into your subconscious mind. And that takes a toll on closeness in your relationships. Because if the condemned parts of yourself were to be exposed and others see it, your Inner Critic would lead you to feel the pain of humiliation. And there's the connection: I have to stay distant from you; can't let you know all of me. If you did see all of me, especially those hidden parts, you would surely reject me. This is why Anthetic Inner Critic work is so crucial to high-voltage soulmate relationships. As you get free from your Inner Critic, as you no longer accept its condemning messages, you move toward welcoming all parts of yourself. And, so you open yourself to letting others see you too. Now you can connect the dots: Self-Acceptance…Closeness.

October 16

Are You Expanded by This Relationship?

There's another way to check for the goodness of the relationship you are in. Jim's 1989 letter to me captures it: "As I was coming from the dentist yesterday, I ran into my favorite school comrade from my master's program. I hadn't seen her since before you and I met. As we talked, I noticed I was more open, more loving, much more boldly emotional. It felt so nice to watch myself enjoying the fruits of yours and my precious relationship, to see the change in me because of you. Your femaleness is so damned good for me!" Can't you just hear the expansiveness in Jim? That's what to look for in yourself. Does this relationship; does my partner open my soul? Am I expanded by this relationship?

October 17

Honeymoon Forever!

The results are in: You Can honeymoon forever! Research from Bianca Acevedo, Ph.D. found that romantic love—yes, you heard it right—romantic love—is an attainable lifetime goal for relationships. Don't think your relationship has to settle into mere companionship. It doesn't. What's more, romantic love is good for you. As Jim wrote me many years into our marriage, "You are my twin; my heart's desire, you set various parts of me on fire…And as we go from day to day in a seemingly quotidian way, the splendor of our lives hold sway, And God looks down to seek—His two lovers."

 # October 18

Should You "Fake It Till You Make It?"

"I'm just gonna fake it till I make it," she said. She wasn't having a good day. In fact, she was in deep emotional pain about a relationship. I told her, "I don't recommend that. In Anthetic Therapy we approach pain relief in a different way. We do Inner Figure work. That means identifying the part of yourself that got triggered and came on stage when you felt hurt by what that person did or didn't do." So, she addressed her feelings in this way. She discovered it was a hurt child part of herself, who felt "not good enough—ever." With that realization, she could orchestrate that inner figure, tell the pain-filled little girl she understood her pain, but she wasn't going to view her relationships from that perspective anymore. As she dialogued with that part of herself, she shifted into her rational Executive Self, who could evaluate the relationship, along with the illusions and expectations she had unconsciously held about it. By the end of the conversation, she was out of the grip of the pain and into a strong, disengaged woman. It was a pleasure to see. So, should you "Fake it till you make it?" Not when there's a better way.

 # October 19

Guilty about Breaking Up?

Are you feeling guilty about breaking up a dead-end relationship? You knew it was going nowhere; in fact, it wasn't good for you. Still, you think you have to pay back or atone for the hurt the breakup triggered in your partner. Don't trust those thoughts. Guilt feelings are simply a form of psychological pain generated by your Inner Critic. If you buy into them, they can disempower you— keeping you in a destructive or unfulfilling relationship. Be at peace. Ending an unfulfilling relationship is a positive growth step. Those backlash feelings of guilt are a sign that you've done it right. You can, of course, feel empathy for your former partner who is in pain. But don't think that you've committed a crime. You haven't. Say to your Inner Critic, "Just because I trigger pain in someone by ending a relationship, doesn't mean I'm a bad person." You are moving forward. Making way for your soulmate.

 # October 20

Got Romantic Fantasies?
You Can Live Them Out

"Now about our wedding ceremony. A pitcher of cream—yes. And a bowl of strawberries. We'll feed each other to symbolize the lusciousness of our sexual communion." Jim wrote this as we prepared for our wedding. Then he wrote, "And let's have a stuffed tiger—as a symbol of our having to defend our relationship against the cynicism of others. I love these thoughts; I love making these plans; I love enfolding our actions in powerful meaning. Yes, we are about to live out our most dear and cherished romantic fantasies." We were determined not to live on automatic; instead to infuse our everyday lives fulfilling our dreams. You can too. It's a matter of choice. So, soulmate quester, go ahead and dream! Then look for a partner who wants to join you in making those dreams come true. And those of you who are soulmates, pull out those old romantic fantasies, dust them off, and live your dreams.

 # October 21

Got an Inner Rebel?

"Why can't you do this simple thing I want?" he asked. She shook her head, "I don't know." As we explored her resistance to complying with his easy-to-do request, an interesting part of herself emerged: The Inner Rebel. She said, "If I do what you want, I'm knuckling under. I had enough of that with my dad growing up. I'm never gonna do that again." Many of us have an Inner Rebel. It's an inner figure whose purpose was to create some power for us when we felt powerless. It can create a powerful pull on us, influencing our behavior without our awareness. In intimate relationships, it can block our ability to express love and caring behavior to our partner. If we follow the pull to respond from this figure, it will harden our hearts to our partner's longings. If you find that your Inner Rebel is sabotaging your relationship happiness, dialogue with it. Tell it whether you want it controlling you. You can have power without coming from a rebellious part of yourself. Once you've disengaged from this figure, your heart will soften toward your partner. Your love will flow.

 # October 22

Stand with the Ecstasy

I don't know about you, but I've had this problem. It's about standing with the ecstasy of someone expressing love to me. In 1989, Jim wrote me that he wanted us to work together, presenting workshops. I put our feelings into this letter: "You were so fearful to say it, and I was so beside myself to hear you offer it, that we both just touched it and ran, like two excited children touching some fascinating beautiful piece of crystal, then streaking off." As more and more opportunities for experiencing the ecstasy of Jim's expression of love for me, my tolerance for the intensity of it grew. I learned to catch myself when I deflected love or touched it and ran. Still when I saw that I missed the opportunity to enjoy expressed love, I learned to say, "Would you say that again so I can let it in?" Today, I pass this idea on to you. Savor the love that's coming your way.

 # October 23

Here's Your Inner Critic Decoder

"I have a hard time identifying my Inner Critic should. It just sounds like me!" This is a common problem, because shoulds frequently masquerade as needs, wants, and "normal desires." One example: "I just don't like to be pushy." That's code for "I shouldn't assert my own needs." When Jim was a little boy, Ovaltine offered a Little Orphan Annie Decoder ring if you sent in so many labels. He was so excited the day his came in. We want to give you your own magical Anthetic decoder. Here's how to tell the difference between a want and a should: If you don't obey the should or shouldn't, you'll feel a twinge or jolt of pain. (That's an Inner Critic emotional punishment.) If you don't get a want, you just feel disappointed. With this in your pocket, you'll be able to solve the mystery of Inner Critic shoulds.

 # October 24

Soulmates Share "Head-On Love"

"I was so blessed that you saw your evasion of facing my feminine power. And that you chose to face me, to hold it. Oh, you are big enough for me. I long for a man to face me head-on on all levels: emotional (you do); physical (you do); intellectual (you do), and spiritual (ah you do). Thank you, Jim." I wrote this to Jim six weeks after we met. I had been revealing my thoughts and feelings to him about his attraction and power for me. It wouldn't have been unusual if he had not responded directly to my words, out of embarrassment or fear. But he gave me a direct, feelingful response. So, how do you grow the capacity for such high-voltage connection? I'll quote my Mama on this one. She told me, "If we say, 'This is too much for me, it often is. But if we say, 'I am big enough to contain this, we can.'" You can do this too. Just resist the urge to avoid a deep connection. Face your partner's feelings. Claim your head-on soulmate love.

 # October 25

Should You Share Your Sexual History?

Okay, it's time we dealt with this one: Should you share your sexual history with your soulmate? Yes, if you want high-voltage closeness. "But it has nothing to do with this relationship," you may protest. Not true. It's part of who you are. Those experiences all went in to making you the person your soulmate loves. When we hold back our history from our partner, whether it's sexual details or emotional experiences, we create distance. Now, it's going to take skill to manage this revelation. Your partner will have to do work to get free from those reactive feelings that get triggered, like jealousy, insecurity, self-doubt. But it can be done. We help couples do it all the time. Plus, we have done it in our own relationship. Be guided by this ideal contained in Jim's words to me: "I bless every sexual experience you've ever had. And I bless every partner you've ever had for whatever pleasure they have given you."

October 26

Indignation: It's a Clue

Do you feel indignant when someone challenges you about something? Indignation is a form of anger. You can feel it sort of swelling of your chest and shoulders. It feels righteous. We want to tell you what it indicates. It's a valuable clue to a fusion inside you. What we mean is you're psychologically welded to the idea, belief, stance you're holding. In short, you're not free. Not free to consider options. Not free to grow. Most important, not free to connect with your partner. Your indignation becomes a suit of armor that prevents closeness. Here's the first step in getting free: Say, "I could be wrong." This will open the door to looking at things objectively and rationally. And it will open your arms to your partner.

October 27

Who's Your Designated Black-Hole Filler?

This is a tricky subject. It's about your Black Hole. That's what we call the part inside us all that yearns for love. It's both a gift and a challenge. The gift? It causes us to fall in love, to seek intimacy, and to want to merge with another person. The challenge? To not let it dominate us so that we choose the wrong partner just to fill it at all costs. It's important that we become conscious about who we're selecting to fulfill our Black Hole needs. Are they free to be involved with us? It's tempting to choose someone who hasn't developed psychologically enough to enter into a serious relationship. Those choices will only produce pain. Instead, we recommend you be guided by criteria that assure that the person wants as much involvement with you as you do with them. So, think about it. Who's your Designated Black-Hole Filler?

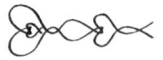 # October 28

Drama Queen: There's One Inside Us All

The Drama Queen. When we see someone who turns every little event into an emotional "Titanic," we feel amused, superior. Yet, inside each of us is an Inner Drama Queen (or King). It's the part that, when faced with daily challenges, becomes anxious, panicky, and worried. It was installed by our parents (and others) who threatened us with our own personal bogeyman. Then they told us all the scary things that could happen to us—especially, if we were to separate from them. Now all those magnified fear messages are echoed by our Inner Critic. "Don't try anything new;" it says, "nothing will turn out right." There's more: "If you leave this abusive spouse, you won't be able to find anyone better." "If you go to that party, no one will talk to you." "If you speak your voice, no one will love you." Each of these is concocted by your Inner Critic to make you feel so scared, you'll stay in the constricting boundaries it has set for you. To be free from the drama of all this, do 3 things: 1) Label your worry and anxiety--"That's my Inner Drama Queen, fueled by my Inner Critic." 2) Get free; "I'm not going to trust those negative predictions for an instant. They're meant to keep me in a cage." 3) Tap your inner power. "I am a person of power. I have the resources to face this and triumph." We're backing you all the way.

October 29

How to Answer "A Penny for Your Thoughts"

"A penny for your thoughts." Boy, do we make this one complicated. Some people reply, "Why do you ask?" Others say nothing. Still others say, "Why do you always have to ask me that?" It's really quite simple. When your partner asks you, "What are you thinking?" just be guided by your values. If you love connection and closeness; in other words, a high-voltage relationship, your response will be, "I was thinking this…" Then you'll give the details. Jim spoke it so well, when he told me his qualities in an early letter to me. "I will always answer if you ask, 'What are you thinking about?'" So, soulmate quester, add this one to your criteria list.

 # October 30

Feel Reluctant? Here's Why

"Oh, I just couldn't bring myself to do that." That's called reluctance. We want to decode your feelings of reluctance for you. When there's something you'd like to do; for example, make a request of an "important" person, but feel you couldn't do it, that's almost certainly your Inner Critic putting the other person on a pedestal and taking away your rights. Now that you know, you can get free. Take back your rights. "I have the right to ask this thing, do this thing, even with this 'important' person." Today, go forth free and in your power.

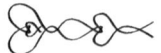 # October 31

Are Your Watchers Haunting You?

It's Halloween in America. A holiday celebrating all things scary. I want to alert you to your own personal Halloween of which you may be unaware. Beware of the Watchers. They're the ghosts of powerful people from your past for whom you may be unconsciously performing. Here's a test: Do you give your partner what he or she really wants—like acknowledgement, sex, affection? Or are you knocking yourself out doing things your partner really doesn't care about—like cleaning the house, leaving no dirty dishes in the sink, or working long hours for extra pay? If you answered Yes to the latter, you may be living your life trying to please the Watchers—people you carry around in your head whose potential disapproval you're trying constantly to prevent. This Halloween banish those ghosts. Here's how to break the spell: Say to your Watchers, "I'm not here to live up to your expectations!"

November 1

You Can Bless Each Other

Are the challenges of this week weighing on you? You could use a blessing. One that sends you forth into the world in the arms of love. As Jim and I parted following our first lovemaking, I wrote him these words: "You are my love, my heart. I, as your priestess, invoke God's blessing upon you—a blessing of safekeeping, of inspiration, of empowerment, of going forth enfolded and of returning to me speedily." You, too, can be priest and priestess to each other today. Reach inside and tap God's love. Let it bless each other. Your burdens will be lightened. You'll walk in love.

November 2

Have You Seen Your Soulmate?

Recognizing your soulmate is going to take preparation and alertness. This is no time for fuzzy thinking. Clear your vision by being specific about what will fulfill your deepest longings. Think in categories. Jim can be your model. His letter to me, five weeks after we met was full of details. "Here's a list of things you give me that are such that I would never leave you. First, your spirituality. It's raw and pure—experiential and powerful. Second, you are in my field. You give me input. We can work together. Then, you are emotionally literate. You can talk about feelings. And then there's the fact that you take the initiative. You call me. You suggest things. Also, you are a vibrantly sexual woman. Lushness, voluptuousness, tenderness, fierceness—all combined. Also, you inspire my creativity. You trigger ideas in me. I wouldn't dream of giving this up." I think that last line is the key. Can you say about this person, "I am so fulfilled by you, I wouldn't dream of giving this up"? When you can say that, you know that you have seen your soulmate.

November 3

Are You Afraid to Ask for What You Want?

Bologna. That's what I wanted. It was our first grocery shopping trip together. Jim went for the ham and put it in the basket. We pushed our cart on to the next aisle. Jim saw I was upset. He said, "What just happened?" I said, "I wanted bologna!" He said, "We both get to have what we want. Did you think you couldn't say what you wanted or just pick it up?" I said, "Yes." Boy, that was early in our marriage, and I had a lot to learn. More to the point, I had a lot of self-constriction to overcome. All those inner critic shoulds not to say what I wanted. If you have that too (and most of us do), realize it's just your Inner Critic saying you don't have the right to say what you want. It may even tell us that our partner will get angry if we make a request. What's needed is an Anthetic challenge. Here are a couple: "I have the right to say what I want." "Even if my partner gets angry, I still have the right to make this request." Now you've got it: If you're afraid to ask for what you want, that's just your Inner Critic. Label it. Challenge it. Your satisfaction will grow.

November 4

A Skill for Protecting Your Relationship

"Please, darling Kathy, sharpen your critical thinking skills so you can do battle with anything that may threaten anything we have created." I was going to a conference, and Jim was concerned that I would hear a lecture that presented some cynical ideas about love and closeness. He was right. They did. He was afraid some negative influence would threaten our relationship. It did. I called him from the conference, shaken by some ideas I'd heard that discounted love. That's when Jim started teaching me the skill of critical thinking. This skill entails asking, "What might be wrong about this idea? What might be right?" You'll need some standards, concepts, and values with which to evaluate those ideas. Jim laid them out for me, and we are laying them out for you here. Is this idea supportive of inner freedom, love, connection, caring, closeness? You'll easily answer "Yes" if the ideas presented are supportive of your soulmate relationship. Critical thinking is an essential skill for protecting your relationship. If you value your relationship, you'll say, like Jim did, "I feel like a Daddy Tiger whose mate and cubs are threatened by outside forces and who will fight to the death to defend them. Oh, I hold you so close, hug you so tight!"

November 5

Do You Feel as Though You Don't Belong?

It's already starting. Those holiday crazy feelings. There's one in particular our therapy clients are beginning to struggle with—feeling as though you don't belong. "Everybody else at the party or the family dinner has a right to be there, but not me!" We want to tell you not to trust such feelings. They're sheer Inner Critic messages: You're defective. Inferior. Not a full-fledged member of some group. Or even of the whole human race. It's your Inner Critic that's labeling you "the Outsider." We're here to empower you to be free from that inner saboteur. Say to your Inner Critic: "I have the right to be here. I have the right to be *what you call* defective and inferior and *still* be here." Claim your place at the party. At the table. You are welcome here.

November 6

Lie Together Like Puppies

Bubbles, the sweet maltipoo, brought her puppies to visit! Two little adorable fluff-balls. Watching them playing and sleeping is a lesson in love. They are all over each other. When nap time comes they sleep on top of each other—full body contact. We can learn from them how to draw maximum warmth and closeness from our partner. Jim and I observed after we'd lain together for the first time: "Remember waking up in the night and hugging each other as we lay, our naked bodies pressed together, your soft flesh curving into mine, fitting together as though God had made them for that purpose?" So, don't miss out on this gift with your soulmate—lie together like puppies.

November 7

How to Increase Your Empathy

Empathy no-no's: Laughing when your partner gets hurt. Saying, "Don't cry!" when they're shedding tears. Not responding when they tell you they need to talk. If you want closeness, you're going to need to be able to empathize. Why? Because partners need to understand what each other is feeling. That means imagining yourself inside the mind of your partner. What thoughts and feelings would he or she be having? It's going to require giving up self-centeredness in favor of attending to your partner. What can make it hard is your Inner Critic whispering in your psyche that to empathize would be humiliating. You'd no longer be the center of attention. You'd be one down. Don't believe it. To empathize, to care, to understand is the path to a soul connection.

November 8

Are You a Counter-Complainer?

"Well, you do it too!" That's called a counter-complaint. This form of defensiveness is so common, we know you've either seen it or done it or been the target of it. It has a psychological purpose: to avoid responding to what your partner has said. At a deeper level, it's an attempt not to feel Inner Critic humiliation at the feedback you've been given. Even deeper: it's an attempt to win at all costs. When couples engage in counter-complaining, closeness is lost. What can you do? If you're the counter-complainer, monitor your impulse to respond to feedback by doing it, then resist the pull. If you're the target of it, note your pull to go along with the topic switch, then instead say, "You ignored what I just said." This will get you started toward connection. And closeness.

November 9

You Can Weather Waiting for Your Soulmate

The soulmate quest can be an exercise in patience. And in loneliness. Jim and I know about this. Jim was 59 when we met; I was 37. He had been divorced over 20 years; I had been divorced 13 years. So how do you weather the hours, days, or years of loneliness? Here are two suggestions you can implement today. One, make a list of people you love to be around. Start calling them—maybe just to talk; maybe to make plans to do something. And two, make a list of things to do that give you pleasure—from feeding the birds to going out to lunch to taking a trip. Pick one, and do it today. As you live your life connecting with people who give you pleasure and doing things that make you happy, the hours and years of soulmate questing will be full of a happiness all their own.

November 10

Touch Each Other

We love touch. It is so good for us; producing oxytocin, the feel secure and loved neurochemical. Jim and I decided we would deliberately touch each other every time we passed each other. So, when either of us was sitting on the sofa and the other passed behind them, we would tenderly touch or stroke each other in passing; sometimes on the shoulder or a stroke of the hair or even a soft kiss on the back of the neck. In the grocery store as we shopped together, Jim would push the grocery cart while I tucked my hand in the back of his belt. In the car, if I was driving, Jim tucked his hand under my thigh. In these ways, we always felt connected, loved, merged. You can't do too much touching.

November 11

Be the Friendly Face

Fight, flight, or freeze. Those were the automatic options science used to say were open to us in the face of threat or trauma. Now, new research shows there is one thing we all do before any of those. *We look for a friendly face.* One that says, "I'm so sorry you're going through this. You don't deserve it. I'm here." Such a response quells our panic; helps us center. When we know we're not alone, we can face anything. So today, be each other's Friendly Face.

November 12

What to Say to Your Partner's Old Hurt

I'd been here before; seeing Jim through the lens of an old core hurt from my childhood. It was a trance I'd get into of anger. He'd tried everything to break me out of it—defending himself; approaching me with rationality. Nothing had worked. But on this day, he did something new. In the face of my anger he said, "I can see you're hurting. You don't deserve that. I hope you come back to me soon, because I love you very much." That did it. He saw my hurt. He loved me. He was standing with love. That worked. It melted me. In the face of your partner's old hurt, offer the words Jim said to me. You can quote him.

November 13

Primal Pain & Your Relationships

It comes in waves. Primal pain, that is. It's the pain we carry from our past. All the way back to infancy. The pain of not being loved, nurtured, responded to. And sometimes when responded to, only with abuse. Being in relationships triggers our primal pain. It can happen for several reasons. Maybe we choose the wrong partner, someone who resembles those early pain inflictors. Maybe we see a really good partner through the filter of those earlier relationships. I know I have. One time, I was sure Jim was fussing at me. It so happened we had a tape recorder on. Oh my gosh, when I played it back, his voice was the tender, loving one I knew. I had heard him through the memory of primal pain. What to do about primal pain? Identify the person from your past from whom that pain came. Imagine they're with you, then express your pain and anger as fully as you can. You'll be draining your primal pool of pain. Do it as many times as you need. You'll feel relief each time. Through this process, you'll be able to see your partner clearly. Healing primal pain is your path to happily ever after.

November 14

Do Couples Become Alike Over Time?

You've probably played this game: Watching couples and noting how much they start looking alike over time. Well, research by psychologist Arthur Aron affirms not that they look alike, but that couples who were close began to adopt the traits of the other. In fact, their brains were slow to distinguish their own traits from their partner's. Does this mean you'll lose yourself if you get close? No. The research indicates that it's that you grow in ways you wouldn't have without your partner, expanding your identity to include elements of your spouse. Jim and I say find your twin; use skills for being as close as possible; support each other's growth. Life will be exhilarating.

November 15

Feeling Stuck? Here's Why

Are you feeling stuck? Does every day seem to be the same-old thing? Every relationship ends up in the same dead end? Here's why: You're living by your Inner Critic's commands. It's the part of you that keeps you stuck. So, any feeling or impulse that could enhance your life gets immediately condemned, rejected, and submerged. You've limited your options. In short, your life is constricted. Take heart. You can get free from Inner Critic living. You can start now. Take back your rights: "I have the right to be Tender in expressing love; to be Tough enough to make requests; to be Self-Sufficient enough to manage on my own when needed; to be Dependent enough to seek a heart connection. In fact, I have the right to be expansive; to step out into my life in whatever way I choose." There! Do you feel your spirit uncramping?

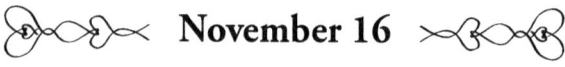

November 16

Are Your Upset Feelings Just "Natural"?

Do you say, "It's just natural to be angry"? Or "Who wouldn't feel bad in those circumstances"? Or even, "It's normal to want your own space a lot"? That's conventional wisdom about emotional pain. But that's not what we say in Anthetic Therapy. Sure, such feelings are common to us as humans. But they're not something we just have to live with; nor just wait until they pass. Such feelings as anger, an impulse to distance, and other painful feelings are clues to a reactive structure driving those bad feelings. Most often, your Inner Critic is pouncing. Then too other inner figures are involved, such as a disempowered figure or an entitled figure. You can take back your rights to analyze each feeling; to get to the source; to get free. You never again have to buy the explanation that your upset feelings are just natural.

November 17

Want to Be Happy? Here's How

Want to be happy? You need to know that your Inner Critic doesn't want you to be happy. It wants you to be safe. Safe from what it sees as dangers of you becoming free. And it's willing to constrict your life in order to keep you safe. That is, what it thinks of as "safe." That Inner Critic-created safety comes at a price. It will tell you to hold back; don't take risks; don't put yourself out there in the world. Once you know this, you can make a choice: Do I want to be safe, or do I want to be happy? If you choose "happy," you'll be choosing to make those connections your Natural Self wants. You'll follow your sparks. We want you to be happy.

November 18

Waiting for Your Soulmate?

Oh, that waiting time for your soulmate can seem like forever. For me, it was 13 years between my first longing and Jim's arrival in my life. But, despite its tediousness, the waiting time is an essential time. Here's how I described it in my early letter to Jim: "You said that you weren't ready for me before. Yes, I feel I have been ripening for you; for our relationship. I am more of a full *me* than I have ever been. I think, 'How strange that this man so perfectly mated to me should come into my life when my life is most full.'" So, soulmate quester, don't despair, your waiting time is an important time for your own development. Use this time to follow your sparks; follow your personal bliss. You are ripening!

November 19

Handling Middle of the Night Worries

Middle of the night worries. Most of us have them from time to time. We want to help you understand, and better yet, handle them. To understand: Such uneasiness comes from your Inner Critic. It pounces when we are vulnerable. Tells us how defective or guilty we are. Or predicts disaster for our plans. What to do: Challenge it. "This is my Inner Critic talking. I'm not going to believe a word it says." We want you to have a good night's sleep.

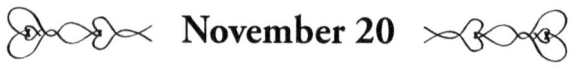

November 20

How to Honor Your Soulmate's Birthday

Today is my birthday. I'm also thinking of all the ways Jim and I have celebrated our birthdays—trips to our favorite places, eating out at our favorite restaurants, shopping for goodies. Recently, I found a letter Jim wrote me on my birthday. It's a model of how to honor your soulmate's birthday: "I want to begin this birthday letter by telling you of my search for you." Then, he traced his almost fifty-year journey seeking me. It was a marvel to read where he was ten years before I was born; the year I was born; how he looked for me in the places he was. "In 1954 (you were 3) I began working in Detroit. If you had gone dancing at the Greystone Ballroom, I might have found you and taught you to dance." In 1985, when you were 34, I had high hopes of finding you in my doctoral program. And then there you were!" He finished with what I mean to him: "You make it all worthwhile. Your sweetness envelops me, your goodness warms me. I love you with all my heart, and your birthday is most important to me. If you hadn't been born, my life would have been incomplete, to say the least." I'm still savoring this decades later. So, when your soulmate's birthday rolls around, try expressing your search and finding of them and what it means to you. Your soulmate will be deeply honored.

November 21

You've Got Fantasy Power

Want to deepen your connection with each other? Try your power to fantasize. Here's an example from Jim and me. In 1989, during our six months spent 2,000 miles apart, Jim wrote me of his hot fever of longing for me. I wrote back from a meditation fantasy I created in order to relax: "There is a peaceful oasis in me—the lush grove deep inside me welcomes you. And there is a little waterfall with cool clear fresh water bubbling. Here, my love, take a drink. And there is a carpet of soft green grass prepared just for you. Lie here, and I will lie beside you. Feel yourself calm." You can do this for each other. Hear the other's distress. Let a helpful image come to you. Speak it, filling in the details. You've got fantasy power. It will bless your partner. And deepen your connection.

November 22

High Self-Esteem: How to Get It

High Self-Esteem: Valuing yourself and having positive feelings for yourself. In our counseling practice, we love to give people the secret to it. I want to give it to you now. We call it Anthetic self-esteem. You can have it by unconditionally loving and accepting yourself. Fear. I accept that. Anger. I accept that too. Awkwardness. I love myself and accept that too. It doesn't matter what comes up, just love yourself and accept that too. You'll walk into your day knowing you're acceptable and loved just as you are.

November 23

Here's the Secret to More Energy

Want to have more energy? We're not going to suggest caffeine or exercise. The secret is in your mind. You just need to get free from your Inner Critic. That's the part of you that saps you of all your Natural Self energy. Start identifying your Inner Critic shoulds, then do a releasing statement for each one. You will liberate the incredible energy within you. You'll experience your own aliveness. We're backing you all the way.

November 24

The Language of Thanks

It's Thanksgiving in America. We tend to focus on the delicious food, the exciting football games, the chance to gather with relatives and friends. Yes, those things are full of pleasure. Yet if you'd like to deepen the meaning of this Thanksgiving, we recommend you speak the language of Thanks. Here are some terms you can use to express the gratitude you feel (they're pulled from Jim's and my love letters): "I am overflowing with joy that you are in my life." "How lucky I am to know you!" "Thank you for your sensitivity to me." "You bless me." "Thank you so much for answering my questions." "You are my gift from God." Oh, there are so many others. But this will get you started. As you prepare for Thanksgiving, let your mind turn to the language of thanks for those in your life. Then speak your gratitude. It will be a blessed holiday.

November 25

Whose Signals Are You Tuned in To?

We're constantly checking for guidance as go through our day. "What to do next", we ask ourselves. So, we tune in to signals. The problem is we often tune in to other people's signals, not our own. It's our own Inner Critic, of course, that drives us to do so. It tells us our own inner judgment is defective, not to be trusted. Theirs is superior. We can stop this process by labeling our self-doubt: "That's my Inner Critic." Then getting free, "I have the right to trust my own judgment."

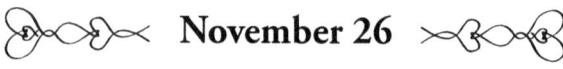# November 26

Are You 2nd Chair at Intimacy?

I'm surveying how I've done at High-Voltage relating with Jim over our 22-year marriage. I feel like I did in middle school when I was learning to play violin. Nancy, my best friend, had the gift. She was always 1st chair violin in orchestra, meaning she was the best. I was 2nd chair. I practiced and practiced. It was hard for me. For her, it just flowed. I told Jim, "It feels like you have been 1st chair High-Voltage Relater. I have been 2nd chair and have had to struggle and practice and practice. For you, it just flowed." He nodded. I'm sharing this because I know for some of you being close comes easy; for others of you it's hard. We want to encourage you. Whether easy or hard, relating to each other with honesty, forthcomingness, and openness is worth it. I don't mind being 2nd chair. Jim is always next to me.

November 27

Your Negativity: What to Do

Judgmentalism, Defensiveness. Withdrawal. All examples of negativity. We know the toll it takes on your dream for a fulfilling relationship. We want to offer you hope—and skills for breaking this pattern. In Anthetic Relationship Therapy, we teach Clue Work; using surface clues such as your negative responses as doors opening into the deeper mechanisms that drive negative behavior. Once you identify the clues, you can dismantle the mechanisms and put them out of play. We're not talking about willpower. Nor trying to shape yourself cosmetically into looking good in others' eyes. We're talking about accepting yourself fully. We call it becoming an Anthetic free spirit. As you get free from self-constrictedness, you'll be in shape for emotional closeness. And for the relationship of your dreams.

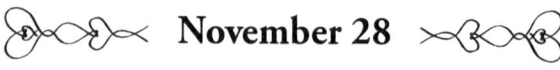

November 28

"Victim Position" Self-Test

Here's a self-test for you. Do you ever say: 1. "You painted me into a corner." 2. "You put me on the spot." 3. "I feel like I'm being punished." 4. "You're not letting me be me." 5. "You're making me into the bad guy!" If you said "Yes" to any or all of these, realize that you've been feeling like a victim. More important, each is a clue to your own power giveaway. We want to help you get free. The secret is that your own should (not the other person's "power") are keeping you in the victim position. The way out? Take back your power by challenging each should contained in the statement you've said. For example, "You painted me into a corner" contains the should, "You should stay where someone wants you to be." The challenge is, "I have the right to go anywhere I please. I have the right to get out of any corner any time I wish." Truth is, you are a free spirit. Claim it today!

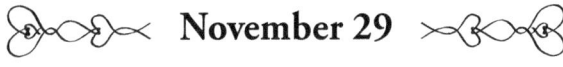

November 29

The One Key to Closeness

You long for closeness. But it often eludes you. And with the very people you love and value. We want to offer you the key. And it's something you can do today. It has to do with coping with other people's intense feelings. Because when you start to get close, those feelings will come up. You'll be tempted to make their feelings go away. Whoa! That's not it. Here it is: Listen to their feelings. Because closeness comes when you are able to let the other person's feelings be what they are and just listen. Try it today. We're with you.

November 30

Envision Your Dreams

I know. It's not Christmas. Even so, visions of sugarplums are dancing in my head. Well, a version of sugarplums. As I read a letter I wrote Jim four months before we married, it suggested how important our ability to image, dream, envision is. Here's what I told Jim: "Thank you for imaging me as a lovely bride. You are incredible, you loving man!" This came after I had told Jim about the wedding dress I'd bought—a Laura Ashley confection of flowers on a sky-blue background. Two thousand miles away in California, he was dreaming of me in that dress on our wedding day. I, in turn, was doing my own dreaming. I wrote, "A little thought: I think I want you to drive the car when we are married." Each of our dreams came to be. Four months later, I stood by him in that dress as we spoke our vows. As we left the wedding reception, he drove. So, our message today is, go ahead. Let your own visions of sugarplums dance in your head. Dreams really do come true.

December 1

Make Your Home a Haven of Love

It was our favorite Christmas rug—a snowman couple snuggled on a snowy hill under the stars. It was such a tender, sweet image that it melted us every time we looked at it. We kept it at our back door to our patio, so we get to see it a lot. We're sharing it with you, because it illustrates an important principle in creating a soulmate relationship. You have to create an environment of enchanted, tender love. And that means beware that your toughness (which can be useful in accomplishing tasks) can block soulmate living. When you surround yourself with these warm, tender images, every time you look at them, you'll get a surge of brain chemicals that bathe your brain in pleasure. You'll be in a frame of mind to turn to your partner in love. And you'll want to communicate to each other in a loving way. So, with that in mind, every time we've seen such images for sale, we've scooped them up to make our home a soulmate haven.

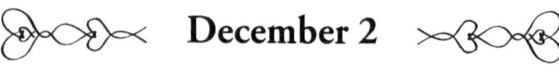

December 2

A Soulmate Addresses Your Fears

Here's one more way to assess whether this person is your soulmate: Does he or she address your fears head-on? With powerful reassurance? That's important. You're going to need to talk about your concerns and insecurities. In response, you need someone who can confront those feelings with soothing words. Take Jim as your model. During our 6-month long-distance relationship, he wrote me: "I want to address two issues (plunging right in), dear one. 'Will he go away because I'm far away?' 'Will he go away because I'm not sexually consummating the relationship?'" He typed this answer in all caps: "I WILL NOT GO AWAY BECAUSE YOU ARE GEOGRAPHICALLY DISTANT. I WILL NOT ABANDON YOU BECAUSE WE DO NOT HAVE A SEXUAL RELATIONSHIP. Period. You may wonder about this now, but you will come to trust it in time." As you analyze what he did, you'll find guidance for recognizing your soulmate. They'll bring up the topic of your fears. They'll be specific about what they see in you. Finally, they'll offer unequivocal reassurance. Now, you're equipped for your soulmate quest.

December 3

I Love That He Makes Me Laugh

I'm recalling the time after Jim's stroke that he looked uncomfortable in his bed. I asked him, "Are you in pain?" His answer: "My hambone hurts!" Me: "Do you mean your bottom?" He: "Yes." As I helped him change positions, I said, "You are so cute! You make me laugh." That got me thinking about how much I loved Jim's sense of humor. He made me laugh everyday of our marriage. And I'm not the only woman who likes this in a man. Research shows that in the top five things women like in a man, humor is #2. (Being powerful is #1.) So, men, cultivate the skill of making her laugh. She'll love you for it.

December 4

You Are My Zeus; I Am Your Venus

Venus--the goddess of love. She's by our bed. She's the archetype of free-flowing love. We like that. In a high-voltage soulmate relationship, you're tapping that archetype toward each other. By that we mean, your thoughts and emotions, words and actions express the sort of profound energies associated with the gods. When I looked at Jim, I saw Zeus, the king of Greek gods. Zeus came to mind because Jim held that nobility, power, and wisdom I think of when I think of Zeus. We want to introduce this idea to you. See each other's greatness. Tap your own archetypal energies. It's a heady experience. Soon you'll be living on Mount Olympus.

December 5

The Innocence of Love

"I feel like a little child, trusting and good. Innocent and loving. Facing you." Jim wrote this to me two months after we met. It reminds me that love requires a return to innocence. When we love, we drop our defenses. We open our hearts. Like little children, we have no façade of coolness or toughness. We open our arms. Our faces go soft. Our love freely flows. For high-voltage soulmate love, this childlike loving is mutual. So, soulmates, today, return to innocence.

December 6

Your Flaw Report: What to Do

You probably have a "Flaw Report Filter." It gets triggered when someone gives you some feedback that disconfirms your self-image. Such a filter will make the feedback look like a flaw report; that is, a notice of your supposed defects. Not true. That feeling of defectiveness is an *add-on*. It's your Inner Critic at work, adding a layer of condemnation to what you've been told about yourself. We want to offer you a magical equation that will clear away the add-on: Do Inner Critic work; subtract the add-on. That will equal your ability to listen to any feedback with astonishingly unruffled equanimity. Here's a challenge to your Inner Critic to get you started: "Just because I feel flawed doesn't mean I am. I have the right to be what you call defective, I'm still a good person."

December 7

Are You Attracted to a Cool, Distant Person?

They're cool. They're distant. You feel a rush of attraction. You misconstrue their coolness as a sign of strength. And you're looking for that in a partner. But, wait! At some deeper level, beneath your consciousness, there's machinery clanking away. It's Inner Critic-driven machinery that whispers in your ear, "This cool person is valuable--superior to you. If you catch them, it proves you're worth something." On top of that, your Black Hole that longs for the love of a distant person (like Mom was, or maybe Dad), nudges you with, "Maybe you can convert them into a warm loving person." We're here to tell you: This is a losing game. Conversions of this sort rarely occur. When they do, it's because the person does in-depth work on getting free from the armoring that creates that cool, distant exterior. So, don't trust that attraction you're feeling. Go for the warm, welcoming person in your world. It will save you loads of pain.

December 8

Guilt: Why It's Not Good for You

Guilt feelings. Let's put it bluntly. They're destructive to you. Why? Because they disempower you. Their purpose is to keep you in your place. So you won't get too big for your britches. Keep you from making requests. Not "burdening" others or "intruding" on them. When you're guided by guilt feelings in a relationship, you twist yourself into a pretzel. Can't say no. Can't express who you are. Then you start feeling trapped. Suffocated. And very angry. This results in a tragic loss for your relationships. A loss of vitality. The magnificence of who you are gets squelched. What to do? Don't trust your feelings of guilt. Get free from your Inner Critic should to be self-effacing. We're here to help you get free.

December 9

Insurance Against Infidelity

They're in deep pain. This couple who comes to see us because one has been unfaithful. She's oh so hurt—and angry—betrayed. He's suffering guilt, even anguish. He's puzzled that he did this thing. How can *you* never be this couple? What we've learned in our forty years of doing therapy is that an infidelity occurs when distance and anger have built up. Instead of talking about the feelings, you act them out. The infidelity is a drama that portrays the pain you're in. It's not conscious, of course. To protect your relationship from this process, you'll need to be vigilant about two things: One, you'll need to be in touch with your hurt, anger, and yearning toward each other. Then talk about it. We know it's scary. We did it throughout our 22 years of marriage--over and over. Two, you'll need to become conscious of the inner figures inside you who are ready at any moment to enact your pain. It might be a petulant child figure or a vengeful part of yourself. Once you know you have these parts, you can feel the pull to let them speak for you. Resist the pull. It would only be trouble. Let your voices speak as neutrally and non-judgmentally as possible what you need from each other. If you'll do these things, you'll maintain your closeness. This process will be your insurance against infidelity.

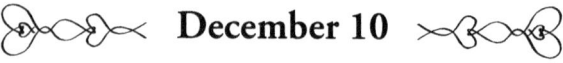

December 10

Are You Irrational? Test yourself.

Are you irrational? Do you say: 1) "I don't need to do any psychological work on myself in order to have a romantic High-Voltage Relationship. All I need is love." 2) "In choosing a life partner, I don't need to use criteria; I just need to ask myself is this the real thing? Is this true love?" 3) "If a thing feels right in my gut, I'll do it, even though I wonder if it's really good for me." If you answered yes to each of these, that's a clue that you're thinking in an irrational manner. It's a form of magical thinking. This is emotional seepage. Your emotions seep into your rationality and contaminate it. Seepage leads to unreflective decisions. You may marry someone impulsively, only to find out later she's just like your controlling mother. Or he's just like your remote father. Instead, we recommend you cultivate rationality. That is, be guided by your Rational Self, who considers the pros and cons of any choice. The Rational Self has well-thought out criteria for guiding your decisions. You'll still have magic in your life. It will now be included when you've assessed that no negative consequences will result from it.

December 11

When Your Partner Is Hurting

"I'm beginning to see that when you're feeling hurt and insecure, I need to comfort and protect you. When you're needy, my own stuff gets triggered, and I wonder if you love me; but it's just that you're feeling bad. So, I'm learning you. I love to make you feel secure-secure in my love, my caring, my help, my confidence. I intend to go on doing that." That was Jim in 1989, learning how to relate to me when I was in pain. You'll want to know what to do when your partner is hurting. You don't have to reinvent the wheel. Jim has shown you how. Comfort. Speak words of protection, caring, and reassurance. Even to the end of his life, despite Jim's stroke and its effects, when I was in pain, Jim said, "Everything's going to be okay."

December 12

The Secret to a Well-Loved Wife

We woke in the wee hours. I told him, "You're my beloved husband." He said in turn, "You are my well-loved wife." I melted and said, "You are right!" I told someone recently, "You have the look of a well-loved woman!" She took it in stride, "Yes, I am." Now, how do you get a well-loved woman? Here's the secret: You make over her. You tell her how much you love her. You shower her with affection. You assure her she's the best. The only woman for you. You'll never leave her. You know what makes her happy, and you do those things. You'll see. She'll walk around with a glowing, happy look that everyone will notice.

December 13

Is Your Relationship a Spy Story?

"I live like a spy in enemy territory--Don't give anything away, because they might get you. I give partial responses. Jim asks for more, and I grudgingly give it." I found this in a journal entry I wrote a number of years ago. It was a pattern I'd gotten into. Play it close to the vest. Jim asked me, "Tell me more. Don't just give me a short answer. Don't be silent for long stretches. Don't shut down. Don't shut me out." As I analyzed my stuff, I realized I had an Inner Critic should to be a perfect wife, with no pathology. I held back on revealing myself in order to obey this should. Perhaps you can relate to this. If you, too, live your relationship like a spy, revealing little to your partner, you can change. It takes an attitude shift. Ask yourself, "Do I want to be self-protective and wreck my relationship? Or do I want to have the right to make mistakes and correct them?" There's nothing wrong with that. It happens all the time. Join me. Come out of the cold.

December 14

"I Like Pats Too!"

After his stroke disabled the left side of his body, Jim's right arm had to do all the loving. When I'd first greet him in the morning, I'd say, "You're my James. I'm your Kathryn. And I love you with all my heart." He reached for me with his right arm and held me tight and patted and patted and patted me. I loved it. One morning, when he woke up, Jim said to me, "I like pats too!" So, as we sat together that night, I patted and patted and patted him. He loved it. My point is what you give your partner in the way of affection and love may very likely be what you would love to receive. You just need to do like Jim did: Tell your partner. That's the thing that makes a high-voltage relationship so satisfying. You think it. You feel it. You voice it.

December 15

Frantic? Here's Help

Do you engage in Frantic Talk? Here's a self-test: Are you tense and high-strung like a spirited race horse in the starting gate? Do you respond with kneejerk reactions? Do you interrupt your partner a lot but have trouble being interrupted yourself? If you said Yes to these, you are driven by a should to react quickly. I had this problem, so Jim taught me some releasing statements I've found helpful: "I have the right to take my time. I have the right to postpone speaking as long as I want. Several minutes. Or hours. Perhaps a full day. Or even longer." We are indebted to Recovery, Inc. for another way to slow down. When frantic, you are *working yourself up*. What you must do is work yourself down. Say soothing things to yourself, such as, "This isn't a tragedy;" "This isn't the end of the world;" "This too will pass." Equipped with these, you'll access you Executive Self for wise decisions. We wish you a peace-filled day.

December 16

These Values Are Toxic to Relationships

We're going to give it to you straight. If you want a high-voltage relationship, you have to flatly refuse to live by toxic values. These may surprise you: 1) Relationships Perfectionism—it causes defensiveness; 2) Reactive Pride—it makes you touchy and quick to take offense; 3) Thinking it's OK to Act Out Negativity; anger, secretiveness, harsh criticism—it will wreck your relationship; 4) Living in Your Little Boy or Little Girl—you'll feel like a victim with no power and see your partner as the powerful parent. If you've gotten into any of these, we want to set you free. You have a choice. Values are chosen. What you choose is what you get. Instead of these toxic values, choose love, psychological flexibility, forthcoming-ness, and working on your stuff. You'll be laying the foundation for an optimal high-voltage relationship.

December 17

Do You Have to Have Faith in Order to Find Your Soulmate?

"I just don't think I'll ever find my soulmate. Do you have to have faith in order to find your soulmate?" It's a question people often as us. From personal experience, our answer is "No!" Doubt is just the result of magnified fear delivered by your Inner Critic. And you know what? Your Inner Critic does not have the power to block your soulmate's arrival. I had lost all faith that I would find a man who would fulfill my heart's desires. I was cynical. But, when I walked into that room the first day of my doctoral program, there was one man sitting there. I saw him in profile. He looked intelligent, wise, strong. I thought, "Looks like a psychologist. Probably wouldn't be interested in me." Hear that? My Inner Critic was *still* insinuating doubt in my mind. It didn't matter. Ignoring the 14 other empty chairs in the room, I made a beeline for the chair right next to him. That was Jim. And he was my soulmate. So, if you want to learn from my story, look at my state of mind. I was doubting all the way up to the moment I saw him. That didn't stop our finding each other; nor our falling in love, not even our marrying. And it couldn't stop the profound fulfillment of my deepest longings. So, we say, faith or not—your soulmate is coming.

December 18

Christmas Ghosts May Be Haunting You

Christmas Ghosts. We're talking about the old feelings of defectiveness and inferiority that get triggered when you're around family and old friends for the holidays. One that's on our minds today: "I have to prove to them I'm good." Variations on this theme: "I have to prove I'm not inferior." "I have to show them what I've made of myself so they'll respect me." We want to assure you this is just Inner Critic stuff. Whether or not those folks are being judgmental toward you, it's your Inner Critic that's delivering the emotional pain you feel around them. Feeling flawed and less-than come straight from that inner torturer. Now that we've given you the label for those feelings, apply it. Every time you feel the chill of those old ghosts, say, "That's just my Inner Critic. I have the right not to prove anything to anybody. My worth is a given; not an item to be proved." We wish you free and happy holidays!

December 19

**Holiday Blues Antidote:
Soak Up the Love**

Holiday blues can hit anybody. We want to offer the antidote: Soak up the love that surrounds you. By this we mean, let in the love of the people in your world who love you unconditionally. Focus on how much they value and love you instead of those people who undervalue you. Open your eyes to the look of love on their faces. Let in their words of kindness. Relax into the warmth of their hugs. I got to experience this at every December commencement day at the university where I taught. As fellow faculty and graduating students talked and hugged, I just basked in all the love we shared. But what's interesting is that after the ceremony I ran errands. As I went from store to store, people were so friendly, sharing greetings and little warm comments. I let in the love too. So, don't miss it this holiday season. There's love all around. I want to tell you that Jim's and my unconditional love goes out to you this holiday. We want you to bask in it.

December 20

Holiday Blues: The Power Antidote

There is a fundamental principle that is the antidote to holiday blues: You have power! We mean personal power to create the holiday for which you long. You are an adult. You have the power to do just what you want to do. Realize this and exercise your power to give yourself pleasure. Follow your sparks. Whether it's making popcorn balls or feeding the squirrels or going to a Christmas concert or simply calling a friend, when you follow even the tiniest spark that promises pleasure, your holiday blues will begin to diminish. You'll warm your own soul. We wish you an experience of your own power today.

December 21

Want to be Surprised this Christmas?

We want to alert you to a stumbling block that could color your Christmas with unhappiness. It's the problem of *symbolic surprise* expectations--those almost universal longings in us that get triggered at holiday gift time. These come from one place inside: our hurt inner child. That child's history included Christmases where we were not seen and heard. Now, we secretly want others automatically to know the longings of our heart for a certain gift. We want the beholding and love we never got as children. Problem is when we try to get what we want by wishing, hoping, and not telling anyone what we want, we are trapped into trying to symbolically fulfill those old longings. How do you get out of the pain of symbolic surprise? The key is to choose to live from personal power. Make the choice no longer to be a silent, disempowered child. Instead, make neutral requests for what you want. And tell the gift-giver how important it is to you. But what if there's no one in your life now to be the gift-giver? Give it to yourself! With an attitude of love and indulgence. You can be the loving adult in your own life. Let the surprise this Christmas be the experience of living from your own power!

December 22

Holiday Frantic? What to Do

It's December 22. They're reminding us, "Only three more days till Christmas." It's enough to get you feeling frantic. Have I bought enough? We want to help you with this. First, recognize that the holidays offer our Inner Critic a perfect opportunity to impose shoulds on us. You know those thoughts and feelings that surround Christmas: gift shoulds, relationship shoulds, activity shoulds. As we say in our book, *Disarming Your Inner Critic*, you have to realize the Inner Critic only has power if you believe it. Our guidance to you this holiday is, Shed the Shoulds! For starters, take back your rights: "I have the right not to buy anything else." "I have the right not to visit; not to stay longer than I want." "I have the right only to do what gives me pleasure." There. You're on your way to peace.

December 23

New Holiday Relationship Skill: Honesty

We began our relationship with a commitment to having as much closeness as possible. As our marriage developed, we discovered a skill that's essential for having closeness at holiday gift-giving time. That skill is *honesty*. What we learned was that being honest with each other about what we like and don't like, whether food item, gifts, or activities, is what creates closeness. And I learned it the hard way. I tried to do the conventional holiday attitude; that is, dishonesty in the guise of niceness. And what I learned is that all that gets you is distance. If you want closeness, you'll need to say, "I choose honesty over distance and over avoiding an argument. We'll learn how to neutrally tell each other what we honestly like and dislike."

December 24

Christmas: For Better or Worse

Yes, the child in each of us comes out at Christmas. That's a good thing, when we get in touch with childlike joy and wonder. It's painful when it triggers all the disappointment, pain, and heartache that our childhoods held. If we will analyze and label and talk about those old childhood hurts, we can become free of their power to steal our happiness. When Jim and I started to consider what traditions we'd create as a couple, I wanted to create a Christmas like my childhood, where there were lots of surprises and I got just what I wanted. For Jim, surprises meant waking up to finding out his alcoholic father had spent his check on liquor and so could only afford an orange in Jim's stocking. As we talked about what we each needed we decided we'd shop together and get just what we each wanted. That shopping held wonder and joy, the fulfillment of our heart's desire. We spent Christmas Eve reading a favorite Christmas story to each other; Christmas morning cooking together and singing Christmas carols. You, too, can forge a Christmas tradition that frees you from Christmas wounds. Talk about the worst of your Christmas experiences. Realize that today you have the power—the power to create a Christmas that's best.

December 25

Don't Scrooge Your Love

They taught me, "Don't put yourself out there for people;" "Make sure you're getting as much as you're giving." I've been evaluating that philosophy I was handed. My conclusion is, "That's not love. That's bookkeeping!" In fact, being in a December frame of mind, I'm thinking, "That's a 'Scrooge' way of living." It's driven by an Inner Critic should for justice. When I live this way, it just blocks love. And happiness. This holiday season, I choose openheartedness and freedom from constrictedness. When I express the love that's inside me, it's bliss. Join me. Don't Scrooge you love. We'll make this the season of joy.

December 26

Those Body Insecurities: What to Do

We want to talk about some pretty core insecurities we've dealt with in ourselves. (Our therapy clients have admitted struggling with these too.) Kathryn: "I think my thighs are too fat!" Jim: "Do girls really like penises?" Because Jim and I wanted as much closeness as possible, we explored these shameful areas with each other. What we discovered is that when you love someone with a high-voltage soulmate love, you embrace all parts of your partner. What has been rejected by previous partners is enfolded by your soulmate. So, Jim told me, "I love your thighs." I told him, "I treasure your penis." Our acceptance of each other is a product of two things: Utter valuing of each other and getting free from any judgmentalism that society can install in us. Once free, you can fully let in your partner's love.

December 27

Reach Out and Touch

A reach-out occurs when a partner overcomes pride and fear and reaches for connection with the other person. In turn, for optimal relating the partner who has received the reach-out accepts the reach-out with a warm welcome such as "Mmm. That feels good that you're reaching out to me" or "Aww. I'd love to have you join me." Such seeking of connection is essential for creating happily ever after.

December 28

The Power of Your Word

"Our Word backed by the power of our assertiveness and our love and intention shapes what happens." Jim's encouragement to me that I was not the victim in my life. In fact, I had, and we as a couple, had great authority in our lives. As the old year is passing, and the new year lies before us, let us take Jim's words to heart. We can shape what happens.

December 29

Beholding: Soul Satisfying Skill

"I love you because your little breakfast is so cute!" I still have this handwritten note from Jim. He'd left it sitting next to my bone china coffee cup I'd placed on the counter ready for my hasty early morning departure for work. When I found the note, I was melted and charmed. He'd noticed! And taken in that despite expecting to be in a rush, I'd still prepared my prettiest cup to drink my coffee from. What Jim did is the skill we call *beholding*. It's when you see your partner in depth. It's in contrast to glancing, in which you note that someone is there but don't take in any details about them and definitely don't speak to them of what you see and love. To behold your partner, here are the steps: 1) Observe your partner in detail. 2) Contemplate with respect and awe what you see. 3) Speak; telling your partner what you see (e.g., "What I love about you is…"). Daily beholding sets the climate for happily ever after.

December 30

Tomorrow Is New Year's Eve: On the Cusp of Change

Tomorrow is New Year's Eve. An archetypal moment. At its heart, it's about being on the cusp of change. I am meditating on one special New Year's Eve. It was 1988. I was getting on a plane in my home town to fly to San Jose, California. What I knew was that I was on my way to start my doctoral program. What I didn't know was that I was headed to the fulfillment of my destiny. Likewise, for Jim. He was starting to pack for the following week's event—his inaugural doctoral program colloquium. What he didn't know was that it would also be the realization of his heart's desire. That doctoral program was going to be the nexus for our meeting. I just marvel: "Little did we know that we were about to find each other." Perhaps you too have had moments like that. Perhaps this New Year's Eve you are on the cusp of change. May the coming year be the fulfillment of your heart's desire.

December 31

Jim's Blessing to Us

As this guide comes to its last entry, it seems perfect to share with you Jim's letter to me written four months before we married. He closed his letter with these words, "I pour myself out to you. I touch the divinity in you and release my divinity to you—core to core, divine center to divine center. We melt into each other at the very center from whence the whole world was made, from which it is now sustained second by second, where aliveness gushes forth through us, ecstatically, poured out into the world to enrich it, to bring joy, to bring pure love." This is Jim's blessing to us. I offer it to you as you continue your epic journey to happily ever after. Be assured that the love you seek comes from a deep and divine source. It flows to us like an artesian well. And it flows to you.

Happily
Ever
After

Acknowledgements

I love how the books Jim and I have published have been called into being by the loving people who have crossed our path. We could not have shared the thoughts in this book without the incredible contribution of our dear friend, Marianne Prejean. Marianne, your treasuring of the Soulmate Skills blog and your printing each post saved this book. Without you, when the website crashed, these thoughts would have been lost. Thank you from the depths of my soul. To our cherished friend, Linnette Abshire, deepest gratitude for always providing support, love, and wise input on content. To our precious friends, Tamra and Jacob Griffin, we have been richly blessed by your love for us, for Anthetic Therapy, and for using it as a guide to your own fulfillment. Your thoughtful counsel has been invaluable to me on this journey. To our soulful friend, Diane Dodt, we thank you for your enchanted responses to all we have offered. You affirm and inspire us. I want to thank my parents, J.B. and Lorraine Shoemake. Though you have passed from this life, I carry the warmth of the loving romance you shared always in my heart.

About the Author

Kathryn Elliott, Ph.D., LPC-S, is a Licensed Marriage and Family Therapist, retired Associate Professor of Counselor Education, and Director of Anthetic Therapy Center. At age 37 she entered her doctoral program in Counseling Psychology. It was on the first morning of that program at Asilomar Retreat Center on the Pacific Ocean that she walked into the meeting room and found one man sitting there. He was James Elliott and was to be her soulmate. James was the creator of Anthetic Relationship Therapy, an approach he had developed over his 40 years of work with groups and couples in Berkeley, Palo Alto, and San Francisco, California. Over the subsequent 22 years, James and Kathryn through their research and practice developed the High-Voltage Relationship model. Together they lived out their own high-voltage soulmate relationship until James's death in 2011. They are the authors of *Creating Optimal Relationships: Use of the Voltage Concept with Couples*; *Hearts Entwined: The Love Letters of Therapist-Soulmates*; and *Disarming Your Inner Critic*.

For More on Creating Your
Happily Ever After

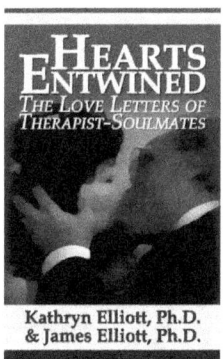

Available through Amazon.com or
Call (337) 450-9910 (Anthetics Institute Press).

www.ingramcontent.com/pod-product-compliance
Lightning Source LLC
Chambersburg PA
CBHW050612300426
44112CB00012B/1476